Building and Managing E-Book Collections

A How-To-Do-It Manual for Librarians®

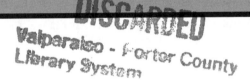
Edited by Richard Kaplan

HOW-TO-DO-IT MANUALS®

NUMBER 184

Neal-Schuman
An imprint of the American Library Association
Chicago   2012

Printed in the United States of America
16 15 14 13 12   5 4 3 2 1

Extensive effort has gone into ensuring the reliability of the information in this book; however, the publisher makes no warranty, express or implied, with respect to the material contained herein.

ISBNs: 978-1-55570-776-7 (paper); 978-1-55570-863-4 (PDF)

Library of Congress Cataloging-in-Publication Data
Building and managing e-book collections : a how-to-do-it manual for librarians / edited by Richard Kaplan.
     p. cm. — (How-to-do-it manuals ; no. 184)
   Includes bibliographical references and index.
   ISBN 978-1-55570-776-7 (alk. paper)
   1. Libraries—Special collections—Electronic books. 2. Electronic books. 3. Libraries and electronic publishing. I. Kaplan, Richard, 1954–

Z692.E4B85 2012
025.2'84—dc23

                                                                                          2012018143

Cover design by Rosemary Holderby, Cole Design & Production
Text design in Galliard and Frutiger Condensed by UB Communications

∞ This paper meets the requirements of ANSI/NISO Z39.48-1992 (Permanence of Paper).

This book is dedicated to the women in my life,
my wife Jane and daughter Chenda,
whose love and support sustain and enrich me.

They also are my best critics
and challenge me to grow and
be a better person, husband, and father.

I am eternally grateful.

Contents

Part III: E-Books in Practice

Example 1. E-Books in a High School Library— Cushing Academy

Tom Corbett

Example 2. Marketing E-Books in a Public Library— Half Hollow Hills Community Library

Ellen Druda

Example 3. Circulating E-Book Readers— Texas A&M University at Qatar

Carole Thompson

Preface

Today libraries continue to move ever more rapidly away from print because users want all things digital. The whole process of selecting, acquiring, and maintaining e-books is very different from the print counterpart. E-book selection and management can be very complex, as three quite basic examples demonstrate:

1. Options now exist for leasing versus owning titles.

2. Pricing can be determined by the number of concurrent users needed, as well as by the size of your user population or community.

3. Publisher and aggregator licenses will determine how you can use, or not use, particular e-books, as well as which titles can be downloaded onto e-readers or smartphones.

Building and Managing E-Book Collections: A How-To-Do-It Manual for Librarians is intended to help guide librarians in all types of libraries through the fundamentals of e-book collection development; to offer realistic, best practices solutions for selecting, budgeting, and assessing e-books; and to demystify the maze of purchasing models and licensing options available.

There was a time—not too long ago—when librarians and publishers were not sure if e-books would ever catch on. There was concern about who would want to sit in front of a computer screen to read a book. Why would anyone want to get eye strain reading an electronic book with a clunky interface and poor search capabilities? With early e-books, it was far easier and quicker to use an index in a print book than to try to wander through the maze of keyword searches and electronic tables of contents. Some first-generation e-books were simply scanned PDFs of the print copy, with illegible images and small print.

Fast-forward to the present, and now there is universal acceptance for all things electronic and all things mobile. Clunky interfaces have been replaced, as a new field of engineering has embraced user interface design. Readers can see definitions of words in the text, create notes and bookmarks, change font sizes for easier reading, or listen to their e-book as an audiobook. They now have the option of reading on a computer screen, a dedicated e-reader, a tablet, or a smartphone. Academic users are driving this revolution, wanting to conduct research and read material in their labs, offices, homes, and dormitories. Moreover, educators want remote access to support online courses and complement learning management systems. Even the general public is now buying more e-books than print through Amazon.com.

Most libraries are shifting budgets toward the purchase of e-books and are buying them in increasing numbers. At the same time, the publishing industry is reacting to this shift by trying to develop new pricing and access models to ensure and enhance their profit margins. All of these factors create a fluid and complicated environment.

Organization

Building and Managing E-Book Collections is divided into three parts: Part I, "E-Books in Context," includes three chapters that provide an introduction and history of e-books as well as an overview of the publishing industry and its impact on libraries. Part II, "E-Books in Detail," features specific chapters dealing with all aspects of e-book management, including selection, budgeting, licensing, cataloging, and assessing. Part III, "E-Books in Practice," presents six carefully selected practical examples that offer real-world solutions.

In Part I, the first three chapters offer essential background. Chapter 1, "The Electronic Book—Beginnings to the Present," provides an introduction to and history of e-books and helps to establish a framework for the rest of the book. An overview is presented on the current state of e-books in libraries and some of the differences in their use and acceptance in public and K–12 libraries, as well as in higher education.

Chapters 2 and 3 examine the current state of e-book publishing. Chapter 2, "E-Book Publishing—A View from the Industry," is written from the perspective of an executive at a major book distributor. She examines the dynamic tension of an industry adjusting to new market forces and profit venues and trying to create products that keep up with new, ever expanding, information technologies and consumer demand. Chapter 3, "E-Book Publishing—The View from the Library," discusses the publishing industry from the library perspective. As publishers develop new business models by making e-books available as individual titles or as part of large subject collections with ownership and lease options, the chapter discusses the impact on libraries' budgets and collection development. Also covered is the issue of how publishers use digital rights management (DRM) software to safeguard copyright and access.

Part II begins with Chapter 4, "E-Books in Public Libraries," the first real "how-to-do-it" chapter. This chapter covers the process of starting an e-book collection in a public library from selection to staff training to policy setting.

Chapter 5, "Selecting E-Books," details the selection process, from methods of identifying e-books for purchase, to understanding the many e-book purchasing models now available. Also included is a detailed examination of e-book formats, platforms, and display devices.

Chapter 6, "Licensing of E-Books," describes how publishers and aggregators create legal documents to establish how the library can, or cannot, use their products. This chapter examines licensing variations among different platforms and use models, as well as its impact on interlibrary loan, course reserves, and long-term or archival access. As the different purchasing models and license restrictions are detailed, it becomes clear that each variation has budget implications.

Chapter 7, "Budgeting for E-Books," provides a detailed analysis of the cost considerations for many of the different purchasing models, including title-by-title, subject collections, leasing versus ownership, and patron-driven acquisitions. Also discussed are the cost of adding concurrent users to a subscription and the implications of duplicating print and electronic titles.

Chapter 8, "Cataloging, Locating, and Accessing E-Books," is a comprehensive, step-by-step examination of how to catalog e-books with detailed examples of different MARC records with identification of important fields. Also included is how to make resources available to users, both through the cataloging record and by managing URLs and proxy servers.

Chapter 9, "Assessment and Evaluation of E-Book Collections," covers assessing and evaluating e-book collections, including usage data, overlap analysis, survey instruments, focus groups, and the balanced scorecard method.

Building and Managing E-Book Collections concludes with Part III, six practical examples that offer real-world scenarios and helpful tips for successful implementation in a variety of settings:

1. E-Books in a High School Library—Cushing Academy: This is a description of how a private, secondary school library removed the majority of its print collection and replaced it with e-books. Topics discussed include patron-driven acquisitions (PDA) and using Kindle e-readers.

2. Marketing E-Books in a Public Library—Half Hollow Hills Community Library: Strategies used to introduce and publicize e-books in a public library are examined, including getting staff buy-in and training and marketing techniques, such as establishing book discussion groups, having vendor demos, and creating an "electronic petting zoo."

3. Circulating E-Book Readers—Texas A&M University at Qatar: Discussed is an innovative approach to providing e-readers as a response to a limited availability of English language books in Qatar. The process of establishing and evaluating this service is examined.

4. Changing Library Staffing Models to Manage E-Collections— George Washington University: Managing larger e-collections requires new job responsibilities and skill sets. The author describes staff reorganization and the other organizational changes needed for e-book selection, processing, and cataloging,

as well as tracking license agreements and using electronic resource management (ERM) systems and web applications.

5. E-Book Access Management Using an ERM System—Oregon Health & Science University: The implementation of home-grown versus commercially available electronic resource management (ERM) systems is described. Also discussed are staffing considerations in populating data and maintaining these products.

6. Accessing and Circulating E-Books with E-Readers—Lesley University: This example depicts a small university library's introduction to providing an e-reader service. A detailed discussion of e-reader and e-content selection, access, and circulation decisions, as well as marketing techniques, is provided.

The chapters and E-Books in Practice examples are intended to provide step-by-step guidance for managing e-book collections. The editor and chapter authors hope you will find that *Building and Managing E-Book Collections: A How-To-Do-It Manual for Librarians* provides the necessary information to help you make judicious decisions and ensure successful e-book collection development for your library's users.

Acknowledgments

I would like to thank the Medical Library Association's Books Panel who put out a call for someone to author a book on e-books. Thanks for accepting my proposal.

I would also like to thank Sandy Wood from Neal-Schuman, whose advice and guidance kept me on track and, mostly, on time.

Additionally, I want to acknowledge Joanne Doucette, a trusted colleague and friend, who not only coauthored a chapter in this book but was my informal reviewer and patient listener.

Last but not least, I would to thank all of the wonderful contributors to this book. Your expertise, knowledge, and persistence have made this project a satisfying experience and a worthwhile endeavor.

E-Books in Context

I

The Electronic Book—Beginnings to the Present

Fern M. Cheek and Lynda J. Hartel

Introduction

E-book: the word calls to mind many definitions and impressions—for librarians, publishers, and individual consumers. Several attempts have been made to define the word "e-book" over the years. *Merriam-Webster*'s definition of e-book has remained the same from 2004 to 2011, "a book composed in or converted to digital format for display on a computer screen or handheld device" (*Merriam-Webster*, 2011). Some authors believe the definition of e-book is a work in progress (Gardiner and Musto, 2010). For purposes of this book, e-books will meet the following conditions:

- They are cataloged as books.
- They are accessible via a variety of electronic formats and devices from desktop computers to mobile devices.
- They are born digital (e-book only), or are electronic copies of print books, or are items with the same content as print volumes supplemented with additional content and special features.

Although the notion of computerized books is not new, the modern concept of an e-book is changing constantly. Some libraries and consumers may have a more limited view of what constitutes an e-book, but, as Vassiliou and Rowley (2008) indicate, the definition of an e-book needs to reflect both its persistent characteristics and its dynamic and developing nature.

This chapter provides an overview of the many issues surrounding the history, development, and functionality of e-books and e-book reading devices. As e-books evolve, they present many challenges and opportunities for librarians. The challenges associated with managing e-books in libraries as well as a review of user experiences and requirements are examined.

> "There is great promise and opportunity in the digital-books revolution. The question is: Will we recognize the book itself when that revolution has run its course?"
> —Steven Johnson (2009)

The Transition to E-Books

Rao (2005) boldly stated that the e-book is the most important development in the world of literature after Gutenberg. Certainly e-books are gaining in popularity, for both leisure and educational purposes, but there are many different opinions regarding the e-book movement of late. Consumers are now comparing and contrasting their e-book access options and reader preferences. How and why they choose one access format over another varies considerably from consumer to consumer.

Just as libraries have established large collections of electronic journals, they are now establishing large collections of electronic books. Administrators, librarians, and users alike are advocating for greater electronic collections. In academic libraries, space once used for print stacks are now used for additional computers, meeting rooms, classrooms, study facilities, and more. Librarians have been monitoring their e-book collection usage and studying the preferences of their users. Many studies have found that the preferred format depends on the time, place, and purpose for using the information and that users still prefer a mix of print and electronic books (Hartel and Cheek, 2011; Williams and Dittmer, 2009; Appleton, 2004).

Clearly e-books have come a long way in a short time. Editors of a 2003 American Library Association guide on e-book functionality noted that "since 2000, no single e-book device has thus far captured a significant portion of the market" (Gibbons, Peters, and Bryan, 2003: 3–4). In another 2003 article, representatives from large publishing companies had comments from both ends of the spectrum—one representative commenting that they didn't see e-books becoming a major method of reading books anytime in the next 20 years, while another indicated that e-books would ultimately dominate the market (Hinz, 2003). Fast-forward to 2007, enter the Amazon Kindle. Perfection is in the eye of the beholder, and in this case the Kindle met many of the desires and needs of new e-book users. It offered a lightweight, easy-to-carry reader with features such as a built-in dictionary, the ability to increase font size of reading material, ability to annotate pages, and a large selection of books to purchase. Even with the introduction of the Kindle, a 2009 article stated that "E-books have yet to make a big impact on the general public" (Miller and Pellen, 2009: 1).

In 2011, Amazon provided figures indicating that for the first time it is now selling more e-books than hardback and paperback books (Haq, 2011; Albanesius, 2011). The recent bankruptcy of Borders Group, Inc., has readers, publishers, and other book retailers wondering what the future holds for physical bookstores—both the megabookstores and independent stores. Many in the bookselling business believe that Borders' troubles began when it did not move as aggressively as its competitors on e-book content and hardware (Sanburn, 2011). It may be, then, that the success of all physical bookstores will depend on how they approach the e-book market in the future.

Microsoft declared that 90 percent of reading material will be delivered in an electronic form by 2020 (Yates, 2001). When it comes to e-books, it is difficult to determine just how many are currently available. A review of the news literature shows a variety of conflicting figures. Many articles on this subject include free, out-of-copyright, public domain

Interestingly, based on a Google search, each year from 2009 to 2012, has been called "year of the e-book" by various publishing groups, libraries, and authors.

books in their counts, and others count only what can be purchased. A review of the promotional pages on publishers' websites also provides conflicting information. One figure that seems to be repeatedly used is 10 million, including public domain books (Fleishman, 2010). While the growth of e-books is escalating, it is worth noting that adult paperback books are still the top-selling category of books among all publishers in 2011(Sporkin, 2011).

Advantages and Disadvantages of E-Books

Librarians and consumers alike are exploring their options and weighing the pros and cons of e-book formats. Overall, there are both advantages and disadvantages to using e-books today, and many of these mirror comments presented when discussing electronic journals in the 1990s.

- The advantages
  - Searchability—Readers can search for and find an exact word or subject in seconds.
  - Modification—E-books can be updated more frequently and seamlessly.
  - Portability—One device can carry thousands of e-books.
  - Variety—There are many e-reading devices and handhelds from which to choose.
  - Readability—Readers can increase or decrease the font size of text and the size of images and figures for ease of reading.
  - Value-added features—Many e-books come with video, audio, quizzes, and animation effects that make them more interactive.
  - Space savings—E-books reduce shelving space requirements for libraries.

- The disadvantages
  - Reading on a screen—It is not always preferable to read large amounts of text online; the long-term effect on eyes is still to be evaluated.
  - Battery power—This can limit the amount of time you read or work with an e-book at one time.
  - Security concerns—Digital formats can be affected by viruses and malware.
  - Permanence—Constantly changing devices and content formats bring long-term access of e-books into question.
  - Lack of standardization—Multiple device and e-book formats can confuse readers.
  - Loaning books—Although currently improving, it is still not easy to share e-books.
  - Hidden costs—In academic settings, use of web-based e-books, such as e-textbooks, can lead to increased printing.

○ Direct costs—E-book readers can be expensive for the user. For libraries, purchasing e-books is more expensive than buying print books.

Historical Perspective

It's not possible to discuss the current and future trends related to e-books without considering their colorful past. Many historically noteworthy events have contributed to the e-book market of the present (see the detailed timeline in Figure 1.1). E-book publishers can thank audiobook publishers and providers for creating a nonprint book marketplace. Congress established the Talking Book Program in 1931 and, with the American Foundation for the Blind, developed the first talking books (The National Library Service for the Blind and Physically Handicapped, 2010). With the transition from record albums to cassette tapes in the 1960s and 1970s, the audiobook market grew and libraries became a source for nonprint books. Audiobook access expanded when content transitioned to CDs and again with the advent of the iPod and other MP3 players from 1990 to the early 2000s.

The concept of computerized mechanisms for expanding the way people acquire, store, and process information has been explored since at least 1945 when Vannevar Bush urged scientists to turn their energies from war to the task of making the vast store of human knowledge accessible and useful. He describes a future device, "memex," for individual use, a sort of mechanized private file and library (Bush, 1945). Andries Van Dam, a professor at Brown University, is credited with coining the term "electronic book" while working on early hypertext systems in 1968 (Ardito, 2000; Gardiner and Musto, 2010). During this same time, Alan Kay proposed a sort of laptop computer called the "Dynabook," which he envisioned could be used for reading books (Ardito, 2000).

In 1971, the still-popular Project Gutenberg (http://www.project gutenberg.org/) was born. Michael Hart led the effort to make public domain titles available free of charge to anyone (Ardito, 2000). What began with the *Declaration of Independence* now holds more than 33,000 titles.

As the Internet and World Wide Web developed in the 1990s, the idea of creating and sharing information grew exponentially. This opened up the doors to self-publishing. Of course, it soon became evident that not every resource on the Internet was credible or valuable, but the idea that individuals could publish works on their own and share them with an unlimited audience was quite a phenomenon.

E-book awareness became more prevalent in 1998, when the early devices on which to read the books were developed, including the Rocket and SoftBook readers (Gibbons, Peters, and Bryan, 2003). netLibrary launched its Internet-based e-book service for libraries in 1999, and Google Books was formally released in 2004. Sales of these early handheld devices and e-book collections prompted the publishing industry to take e-books more seriously. Amazon released the first version

The Electronic Book—Beginnings to the Present

Figure 1.1. E-Book Timeline

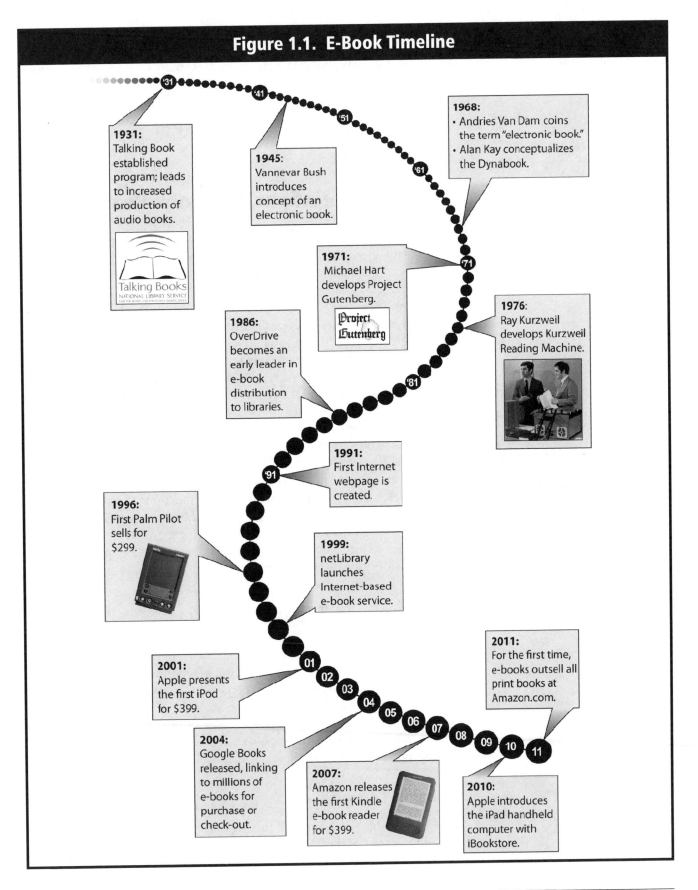

of the Kindle in 2007. Priced at $399, the Kindle first offered nearly 90,000 e-book titles. Since then, Barnes & Noble, Sony, and other companies have followed Amazon with their own handheld e-book readers. In 2010, Apple released the iPad multipurpose tablet computer with e-books available from the iBookstore. Although not a dedicated e-book reader, this device and the popular "apps" and e-book collections have generated tremendous excitement by signaling the age of the multi-use, mobile device.

Current Variations of E-Book Readers

As noted earlier, there are several descriptions and definitions of e-books. Similarly there are an ever-growing number of e-book readers. Marketing to the consumer is increasing with ads on television and in popular magazines, helping to push the demand for e-readers. Advertisements tout the low cost of devices, the types of information that can be read on them, and various device features. These readers are portable devices with technology that allows an e-book to be downloaded and read. Currently the top two selling e-readers are the Amazon Kindle, developed by Amazon, and the Nook, developed by Barnes & Noble (Moon, 2011; Mattingly, 2011). Other notable e-readers include the Kobo and Sony Reader. E-books may also be read on smartphones with operating systems by Apple, BlackBerry, and Google. Tablets such as the iPad and various Android and Windows tablets are really small computers, designed to support multifunctions—listening to music, accessing the Internet, and downloading books to read. Applications, better known as "apps," allow quite a number of these functions to exist. One of the distinctions between these e-readers and tablets is that some are accessible through Wi-Fi, and others, usually more expensive, have high-speed Internet connections, which means that, as with a smartphone, you can use the device to access the Internet if you subscribe to a data plan.

E-Books in Today's Libraries

Libraries are clearly playing a significant role in the e-book content and reader markets. All librarians look for e-book formats that are easy for their particular customers to find and use. Decisions made by librarians regarding e-book content and access are influenced by user populations and associated demographics, library user settings, and purpose of e-book use. Current practices and policies associated with e-book collections can vary depending on these distinctions.

Public Libraries

Much of the e-book growth that appears in the popular press surrounds adult literature, both fiction and nonfiction. Public libraries strive to serve the needs of a diverse population, whose members span the entire

> "I'm sure there will always be dedicated devices, and they may have a few advantages in doing just one thing," he said. "But I think the general-purpose devices will win the day. Because I think people just probably aren't willing to pay for a dedicated device."
>
> —Steve Jobs (Pogue, 2009)

length of the technical literacy spectrum, from those owning e-readers to those wanting to use e-books but need the library to lend hardware.

Making e-book holdings accessible to all users continues be a challenge (*Library Journal* and *School Library Journal*, 2010). The recent *Library Journal* survey indicates that 72 percent of public libraries currently offer e-books to users. As for the 28 percent that currently don't offer e-books, most plan to offer them in the next one to two years. When asked if they circulate actual e-reading devices, 71 percent indicated they do not. Survey authors speculate this is because librarians are awaiting device standardization before entering this arena. Public libraries are analyzing the circulation of their e-books. The *Library Journal* survey respondents indicated that bestsellers, mystery/suspense, and biographies are the top-circulating categories of e-books (*Library Journal* and *School Library Journal*, 2010).

Public libraries are often concerned with and aware of the information and reading needs of the elderly and people with disabilities. E-books and devices can be helpful to these user populations. Read Chapter 4 for a more detailed examination of e-books in the public library.

K–12 Libraries

E-books are starting to gain a foothold in school libraries. The 2010 *Library Journal* survey found that school librarians consider all materials formats and how they fit into their budgets and meet teacher and curricular needs. School librarians noted concerns related to e-books, including pricing and accessibility issues. The survey found that 33 percent are offering e-books and that the likelihood of carrying e-books increases by grade level (*Library Journal* and *School Library Journal*, 2010).

Some of the research into e-book user preferences does not support the notion that younger generations automatically prefer e-books over print—at least not yet (Hartel and Cheek, 2011). While technology is definitely a part of their lives, the technology skills and preferences of young people are not identical. It may be that readers who grow up holding an e-reader of one type or another from a very young age will be more comfortable with e-books, but it does not mean they will automatically prefer e-books or even read more because they are available electronically. Long-term studies of these user populations will inform this debate.

Sharing the same issues as public libraries, many school libraries would like to circulate e-readers to students; barriers include the initial cost of the devices, replacement costs for lost or stolen readers, and the complex selection of readers from which to choose. Many K–12 schools are securing grants and other special funds to purchase e-readers and e-book content. E-reader pilot projects are becoming more popular across the country. Librarians and teachers are willing to explore these technologies if it gets students excited about reading.

Cushing Academy, a private high school in Massachusetts, made a news splash when they eliminated their print books and transformed their library space into a new learning commons model. The E-Books in

---

SOME REASONS THE ELDERLY AND/OR DISABLED USERS MIGHT LIKE E-BOOKS AND HANDHELD DEVICES

- Devices are lightweight: users don't have to haul a big stack of books on their travels or back and forth to the library.
- Users are better able to manage use and access from home: devices reduce the need to travel to libraries or bookstores—for those with physical disabilities.
- Devices offer scalable font sizes and light levels: users can adjust the settings to meet their unique vision needs.
- Many devices offer audio features: audiobook functions appeal to those who prefer or need to listen to books.
- Some devices offer newspaper and magazine options: users are better able to keep up with favorite magazines and newspapers.
- Free Wi-Fi or 3G access: For users without a computer, some devices provide basic Internet access.

Practice section of this book describes the Cushing Academy's transition into a virtual library with e-books (see Example 1).

Higher Education

Just as academic libraries have established large collections of e-journals, they are now establishing large collections of e-books. The high number of students carrying laptops or using the university library computers makes laptop/PC access to e-books convenient. The 2010 *Library Journal* survey found that 94 percent of academic libraries offer at least some e-books. Despite this figure, Levine-Clark (2006) noted that not all college students know what constitutes an e-book. Research has shown that users of scholarly publications tend to prefer and use PDF formats followed by full-text HTML. The open book format, EPUB, used by Apple and other mobile device providers, is also a preferred e-book format among college students.

Many college students still prefer a print book if given an option. This was based on an October 2010 survey conducted by the National Association of College Stores (Young, 2010).

Questions Abound—Forward to the Future

Publishers, librarians, authors, and consumers are all coming together now to discuss important issues associated with e-books. From conferences to blogs and other social media outlets, conversations are taking place that bring these relevant groups together to discuss the future of book publishing and book access. These interested parties are presenting more questions than answers (Gardiner and Musto, 2010). A sample of questions includes the following:

- What, exactly, constitutes a book or what constitutes an e-book?
- Does the combination of new functionalities available in e-books change the definition of book?
- What will we call print books in the future? Will they be p-books (print books) while we flip e-books to just books?
- Will more authors turn to self-publishing in this e-book market?
- What format will our children and grandchildren be using?

As Gardiner and Musto (2010) suggest, the dismemberment and reassociation of content in the digital realm force us to look at these questions in a new light, with a newly focused urgency. Likewise, in his 2001 essay, Clifford Lynch challenges us to think beyond technology gadgets and software and consider the more important issues behind e-books. Lynch believes the future digital book will take us far beyond today's printed books and publishing models—in many different and sometimes unexpected directions (Lynch, 2001).

"The real issues are more fundamental: how do we think of books in the digital world, and how will books behave? How will we be able to use them, to share them, and to refer to them? In particular, what are our expectations about the persistence and permanence of human communication as embodied in books as we enter the brave new digital world?"

—Clifford Lynch (2001)

Conclusion

This chapter examined the rapid growth of the e-book and its related technologies. Libraries generally embrace e-books and have incorporated them into their collections. The remaining chapters will examine the process of creating and maintaining electronic collections in an environment where publishers and third-party pricing models, platforms, and electronic usage rights are in a constant state of flux. Also discussed will be how libraries purchase, collect, and provide access to e-resources, which are inherently different from collecting print. Additionally, this book will look at current e-book issues, trends, and best practices in order to help provide a practical guide for proper selection, budgeting, licensing, cataloging, and assessment of e-books in a variety of libraries.

References

Albanesius, Chloe. 2011. "Consumers Now Buying More Amazon Kindle E-Books Than Print Books." PCMag.com. http://www.pcmag.com/article2/0,2817,2385592,00.asp.

Appleton, Leo. 2004. "The Use of Electronic Books in Midwifery Education: The Student Perspective." *Health Information and Libraries Journal* 21, no. 4: 245–252.

Ardito, Stephanie. 2000. "Electronic Books: To 'E' or Not to 'E': That Is the Question." *Searcher* 8, no. 4 (April). http://www.infotoday.com/searcher/apr00/ardito.htm.

Bush, Vannevar. 1945. "As We May Think." *Atlantic Magazine*. http://www.theatlantic.com/magazine/archive/1945/07/as-we-may-think/3881/.

Fleishman, Glenn. 2010. "How Many eBooks, Ultimately?" PubliCola. http://publicola.com/2010/02/02/how-many-ebooks-ultimately/.

Gardiner, Eileen, and Ronald G. Musto. 2010. "The Electronic Book." In *The Oxford Companion to the Book*, edited by H.R. Woudhuysen and Michael F. Suarez, 164–171. New York: Oxford University Press.

Gibbons, Susan, Thomas A. Peters, and Robin Bryan. 2003. *E-Book Functionality: What Librarians and Their Patrons Want and Expect from Electronic Books*. Chicago: American Library Association.

Haq, Husna. 2011. "5 Signs That E-Books Are Here to Stay." *Christian Science Monitor*. http://www.csmonitor.com/Books/2011/0210/5-signs-that-e-books-are-here-to-stay/New-York-Times-will-add-e-book-bestsellers.

Hartel, Lynda J., and Fern M. Cheek. 2011. "Preferred Book Formats in an Academic Medical Center." *Journal of the Medical Library Association: JMLA* 99, no. 4: 313–317.

Hinz, Christopher. 2003. "Growth of E-Books in Publishing Considered Far Off." *Reading Eagle* (Pennsylvania), November 2. http://www.highbeam.com/doc/1G1-109555784.html.

Johnson, Steve. 2009 "How the E-Book Will Change the Way We Read and Write Source." *Wall Street Journal*, April 20. http://online.wsj.com/article/SB123980920727621353.html.

Levine-Clark, Michael. 2006. "Electronic Book Usage: A Survey at the University of Denver." *portal: Libraries and the Academy* 6, no. 3: 285–299.

Library Journal and *School Library Journal*. 2010. "Survey of Ebook Penetration and Use in U.S. School Libraries." LibraryJournal.com. http://www.library journal.com/csp/cms/sites/LJ/info/Reportpurchase.csp.

Lynch, Clifford. 2001. "The Battle to Define the Future of the Book in the Digital World." *First Monday* 6, no. 6. http://firstmonday.org/htbin/cgiwrap/bin/ojs/index.php/fm/article/viewArticle/864/773.

Mattingly, Joseph. 2011. "Nook Simple Touch May Finally Trump Kindle." HeadlineNews.net. http://www.headlinesnews.net/15734/nook-simple-touch-may-finally-trump-kindle.

Merriam-Webster. 2011. "E-Book." *Merriam-Webster*. Accessed May 25. http://www.merriam-webster.com/.

Miller, William, and Rita M. Pellen, eds. 2009. *Adapting to E-Books*. New York: Routledge.

Moon, Brad. 2011. "NOOK Color Overtakes Kindle." Accessed August 11. About.com. http://portables.about.com/od/ebookreasers/a/Nook-Color-Overtakes-Kindle.htm.

The National Library Service for the Blind and Physically Handicapped. 2010. "Facts: Talking Books and Reading Disabilities." Library of Congress. http://www.loc.gov/nls/reference/factsheets/readingdisabilities.html.

Pogue, David. 2009. "Steve Jobs on Amazon and Ice Cream." *New York Times*, September 9. http://bits.blogs.nytimes.com/2009/09/09/in-qa-steve-jobs-snipes-at-amazon-and-praises-ice-cream/.

Rao, Siriginidi Subba. 2005. "Electronic Books: Their Integration into Library and Information Centers." *Electronic Library* 23, no. 1: 116–140.

Sanburn, Josh. 2011. "5 Reasons Borders Went Out of Business (and What Will Take Its Place)." *Time*, July 19. http://moneyland.time.com/2011/07/19/5-reasons-borders-went-out-of-business-and-what-will-take-its-place/.

Sporkin, Andi. 2011. "Print Books Show Growth While E-Books Continue Climbing, According to AAP Publishers' March 2011 Sales Report." Association of American Publishers. http://www.publishers.org/press/32/.

Vassiliou, Magda, and Jennifer Rowley. 2008. "Progressing the Definition of 'E-Book.'" *Library Hi Tech* 26, no. 3: 355–368.

Williams, Margaret G., and Arlis Dittmer. 2009. "Textbooks on Tap: Using Electronic Books Housed in Handheld Devices in Nursing Clinical Courses." *Nursing Education Perspectives* 30, no. 4: 220–225.

Yates, Emma. 2001. "E-Books: A Beginner's Guide." *Guardian*, December 19. http://www.guardian.co.uk/books/2001/dec/19/ebooks.

Young, Jeff. 2010. "Students Remain Reluctant to Try E-Textbooks, Survey Finds." *Wired Campus* (blog). *Chronicle of Higher Education*, October 26. http://chronicle.com/blogs/wiredcampus/students-remain-reluctant-to-try-e-textbooks-survey-finds/27866.

E-Book Publishing— A View from the Industry

Meg White

Introduction

This chapter provides an overview of e-books from the perspective of the publisher. It also discusses the larger publishing milieu over the past 25 years in order to outline macro issues relevant to the industry as it continues to transition from print to digital.

Solid to Liquid

Publishing has a well-earned reputation as being an erudite, somehow inspired and genteel form of business. Traditionally, it marries the high ideals of knowledge transfer with art and throws in a dash of commerce, just to ensure that the enterprise is self-sustaining. Over the past 25 years, market forces and technology have conspired to interrupt the three-martini lunch in ways that are truly disruptive and transformative: large multinational corporations and third-party holding companies have acquired and merged these formerly small publishing houses (United Press International, 1990), while at the same time technology has fundamentally changed the way information is created and consumed. This is a sticky conundrum; at a time when investment and innovation are required, the expectations for financially based performance have never been higher.

Core Competency and Required Skill Sets

Publishing companies need to reimagine their businesses in fundamental ways, moving from a linear work flow that creates a physical object to a nonlinear content-creation mind-set that creates a liquid—ready-to-pour quickly and easily into whatever container satisfies the needs of a consumer. A 3,500-page encyclopedia delivered electronically in a flat PDF is no more useful than its print analog. Radiologic images presented on a device that does not provide appropriate resolution to allow the user to see a developing tumor is useless. Conversely, information about a potentially fatal drug interaction delivered to a nurse prior to administering a dosage can potentially save lives. But, given 150 years of status quo, this transition is quite daunting, and it requires resources, nimbleness, and focus on core competency and required skill sets. Like a buggy manufacturer in the late-nineteenth century, publishers are coming to the realization that they are no longer in the book manufacturing business, they are in the information business. To make things more complicated, in the days of the printed word, it was acceptable to publish a book and not understand or care how or why the information got used. Old-school publishing was very much about throwing information "over the wall" and hoping for the best. In the digital world, an acute understanding of how a customer uses content is critical in order to produce products that are useful and support evolving information needs.

Evolving Customer Needs

For professional and scholarly information resources, the printed word and memorization have always carried the day. A retired pediatrician reading about the new edition of a classic pharmacology text that he used in medical school, *Goodman and Gilman's Pharmacological Basis of Therapeutics*, was aghast at the price of $129. Upon closer examination he was even more surprised to discover that a book that in his day was 400 pages is now 1,200 pages long, rendering his educational strategy of cover-to-cover reading and memorization impossible. This anecdote illustrates one of the fundamental shifts in the way physicians, other professionals, and even students do their work in an era of an overabundance of information. They can no longer memorize; they are taught strategies and critical thinking skills that allow them to acquire information just-in-time, instead of just-in-case. These evolving information needs mandate a change in how information is used and how information is provided. Rather than page-by-page in a linear textbook, information must come in actionable, digestible chunks, delivered at the appropriate moment. For nonprofessional information resources, with the exception of novels, the same argument holds true.

In the early days of migration from "p" (print) to "e" (electronic), publishers began to develop websites that were based on bestselling lines of text and reference books. The sites, or "portals," would aggregate subject-specific content into a single platform and allowed integrated searching and browsing across an entire collection. Lippincott Williams & Wilkins developed one such site based on their market-leading oncology publications. Demonstrating the new application to one of the lead authors of the anchor text *DeVita, Hellman and Rosenberg's Cancer: Principles and Practice of Oncology*, the author challenged the utility of the electronic delivery; he was very clearly connected to his text, proudly displayed on a lectern in his office. He would search the print index for a topic and in the web application simultaneously and arrive at the same section in the 3,500-page text and at the same moment. "Well, so much for electronic," he laughed. But he had neglected to understand he had just searched not only his book but also the rest of the printed books on the shelf in his office. As much as he loved "his book," when the more comprehensive nature of digital was pointed out to him, his editor never had to discuss the value of "e" with him again. As a physician and a scientist, he understood uniquely the power of access to as broad and deep a pool of information as possible.

Publishing in Transition

This section discusses how mergers have affected the publishing industry as increased revenue became a driving force. Also discussed is the impact of new emerging technologies on the publishing process.

Economic Drivers

In the late 1980s, the Times Mirror Corporation began acquiring and merging small, independent medical publishers. No one took much notice (in the larger landscape of its media empire, these transactions were relatively small), but the acquisitions signaled that the trend of size as a strategy had reached out from big pharma and banking into the gentleman's business of making books. Throughout the 1990s this trend continued, as cash-hungry corporations gobbled up publishing houses with double-digital profit margins. Wolters Kluwer and Elsevier (United Press International, 1990) greatly expanded their holdings of U.S.-based companies with the acquisition of Lippincott Williams & Wilkins, Raven Press, and Mosby Year-Book. And with their new publicly traded status came the need for consistent, sustained financial performance, an acceptable expectation in times of stability. However, with the launch of Marc Andreessen's Mosaic in 1993, the first web browser that featured a "graphic user interface" (GUI), the world of media and communication would begin to undergo changes at a level not seen since Guttenberg. Suddenly, the acquiring corporations were faced with a portfolio of companies in an industry in transition, not the mature, cash-rich properties they thought they had purchased. This need to invest combined with the financial pressures for double-digit growth inherent in a publicly traded company was a recipe for disaster. Publishers were between a rock and a hard place.

Technology Drivers

The Internet not only changed the way people consume content but also had the potential to change the way content is created and delivered. The business of publishing since Guttenberg was about creating a physical object: a book. Operational infrastructure and skills sets were honed and developed to function linearly and produce words on a printed and bound page: manufactured, warehoused, and shipped. Suddenly, new types of content with different utility and the ability to be delivered digitally were possible. Editing tools, work flow support for peer review, controlled vocabularies, and content architecture replaced typesetting and developmental editing. Publishers, still reeling from new corporate financial expectations, saw their well-established processes begin to become irrelevant. And just as they needed investment to reinvent their businesses, the pressure to produce double-digit growth had never been higher. It was a perfect storm. As one CEO described his role in 1998, "This is like turning the *Queen Mary* around in a bath tub." Not an optimistic outlook to be sure.

Customers

The new medium of e-books created an interesting quandary for publishers. For the first time, the customer or user became the principle player challenging the concept of how information is created and consumed.

Intimacy Issues

Into all of the turmoil of publishing over the past 25 years, enter the customer. Customers were always well removed from the professional publishing house; they existed many levels down the supply chain and were occasionally heard from via a stylishly designed direct mail promotion when it was time to order a new book or renew a subscription.

Publishers recognized that their customers existed, but they largely relied on operationally efficient third parties to deliver their content to their users. They had little or no knowledge or need to know about how or why customers actually used their products. As one medical informatist describes this phenomenon, it is the practice of "making books and throwing them over the wall." For words on a printed page, this process was adequate. In the developing world of digital information delivery, it is fundamentally inadequate. To create inactive products, it is essential to understand your users' actions. What information do they need? At what moment? How frequently? What is the role and value of key intermediaries like libraries in the dissemination of information? These questions were only vaguely understood by companies accustomed to little or no customer intimacy.

Shift from Individual to Institutional

The rise of the e-book has been described by a former President of the Medical Library Association as the "Fourth Wave" of digitization: MEDLINE, databases, e-journals, and now e-books. The market changes associated with each phase can inform the subsequent phases, especially e-journals and e-books. Until the late 1990s, journals formed the backbone of the scholarly and professional publishing house. They were prestigious and were highly reliable sources of double-digit renewable revenue from advertising, reprints, and institutional and individual subscriptions. All physicians and scientists kept a library in their office, and they could count on their institution's library for access to the same books and journals when they were on rounds or in the lab. And then the journal was accessible on the desktop, provided "for free," and individuals were suddenly cancelling their personal journal subscriptions in favor of accessing not only single journals on their computer, but hundreds, perhaps thousands of articles provided by their library. The revenue associated with the individual subscription was evaporating, and with it went revenue from print advertising and reprints. A similar situation is playing out with e-books almost a decade later. With journals, the expectation was created that the information a health care professional, faculty member, or student needs to do their work is available on the desktop. E-books have followed journals in this transition. The challenge for publishers is to navigate the shift from individual to institution in e-books more effectively than they managed this same shift in journals.

This trend is also a challenge for public libraries and institutions as they try and keep pace with patron demands as well as new technology. What platforms should they support? Do the business models offered by publishers for the circulation of e-books fit their budget? What about copyright protection? A recent move by HarperCollins to force an additional purchase of an e-book after the title has been "checked out" 26 times (Hadro, 2011) brought great gnashing of teeth in the library world. How did the magical number 26 times get determined? Why is an e-book different from print books that were bought and paid for one time? Will libraries have to begin to "forecast" usage in order to determine their budgets? Many more questions than answers remain, but with each new model, each new stop and start, the landscape is becoming more defined.

More interesting for public libraries and publishers has been the launch of the Amazon (can Google be far behind?) lending library. This program allows users to pay an annual fee and "check out" titles directly from the Amazon Owner's Lending Library. Users can opt to check out titles from their local library as well, for free, if the library has this title in their holdings. This innovative take on the traditional concept of "borrowing" leverages the discoverability of the Internet and has the potential to make content more widely accessible to users. Publishers are paid the full list price for each e-book whenever it is checked out. Seemingly counterintuitively, the reaction from publishers suddenly provided the opportunity to monetize their back list has been met with grave concern and even forceful contention from the Authors Guild (Owen, 2011). How this new model of content dissemination will play out in the long term is still anyone's guess.

E-book access via the institution was codified in very real market terms in 2011 with the acquisition of ebrary by ProQuest (Fialkoff, 2011) and NetLibrary by EBSCO (McEvoy, 2010). Two of the largest and most dominant suppliers of digital content to libraries of all types in the world have acknowledged the arrival of e-books as an essential part of an electronic collection and have moved quickly to add this format to their product offerings.

Is Free Good Enough?

Unlike trade publishing, perhaps one of the most disturbing (or interesting, depending on your perspective) development for publishers of scholarly information is the increased acceptance of "free" information. In the past, the peer-review process ensured the quality and integrity of content. Somehow, in the shift to the Internet, this value proposition has lost some of its luster, and the idea of allowing the "user community" to vet information has gained a fair amount of momentum. Crowdsourcing, or more popularly the wiki, have emerged as reliable sources of information, if not to true academics, at least to rank and file professionals, students, and consumers.

Why pay for the highest quality information if free is good enough? A recent survey of 300 physicians (Wolters Kluwer, 2011) conducted by Wolters Kluwer Health found that 42 percent of respondents "frequently" search for medical information at a commercial search engine—hardly peer-reviewed or scholarly information by traditional definition. Even more than changing technology and unrelenting financial expectations, this trend in the marketplace is perhaps the largest threat to scholarly publishing that exists today.

Supply Chain

The Myth of Disintermediation

In the early days of the Internet, publishers imagined that this new technology would enable them to connect 1:1 with their customers. They envisioned connecting directly with actual end users, bypassing wholesalers, aggregators, agents, libraries, and bookstores. It seemed like the ideal scenario and promised a new era of customer intimacy and potential innovation. The reality of disintermediation as a strategy has evolved somewhat differently in the marketplace, largely due to the fundamentals of the Internet and customer preference. The Internet is about connectivity and access; the publishers' inclination to build walls around their content, creating proprietary islands, is not supported by the integrated DNA of the web. Additionally, customers actually prefer to access and purchase content in a distributed environment. Can you imagine what a bookstore filled with titles only from McGraw-Hill would look like? Disintermediation, like so many other seemingly ideal strategies, turned out to be a better idea on paper than in reality. After a brief period of distraction, most publishers quickly recognized that their future depended on establishing multichannel and multilayer strategies, much more in line with the fundamental nature of the Internet: integrated and discoverable content.

Increased Complexity

So, if disintermediation died in a consultant's PowerPoint deck, what has happened to the supply chain, optimized for print for the past 100 years? Many traditional players have adapted their businesses to include "e" as their customers' needs have changed. Former print subscription agents now offer full-text journals and databases. Bookstores sell via bricks and clicks. Libraries offer federated access to materials from multiple suppliers in a single integrated search, physicians access medical information at the bedside, and the student and the general public have remote access to a world of information no longer restricted to print library holdings. Individuals want instant access on their mobile device. Digital access and web-scale discovery services have transformed the supply chain into an increasingly complex matrix, which must be managed by publishers, with regard to product, customers, and price. What content, what format, and at what price have never been more crucial to publishers' success and never more challenging to balance.

E-Books and the Magic Bullet

Great Expectations

E-books have been facing stops and starts via various delivery devices since the mid-1990s but have begun to gain traction in the institutional market and the consumer market in the past 12 to 24 months. Given all of the turmoil in the market and in the industry, publishers are constantly searching for the magic bullet that will stabilize their rapidly changing businesses and offer a return to the stability of old. In the early 2000s, medical publishers rushed to develop e-books that were designed to run on a Palm Pilot. The revenue was significant, and products delivered on personal devices were by far the fastest growing product line for many companies. CEOs were ecstatic. Do more, they demanded. Unfortunately, by the time "more" was brought to market over the next year, the market had moved on; so much for the magic bullet that would instantaneously save the publishing enterprise. In the current market, publishers are still searching for the magic bullet, and today's leading candidate is the e-book. Unfortunately, this latest savior is no more able to single-handedly resurrect the publishing industry than New Coke was able to revolutionize the soft drink industry.

Apples and Oranges

Usually when we discuss e-books in the science, technology, and medical disciplines, we refer primarily to digital versions of print texts, delivered via the Internet in a browser, often with features that enhance the usability of the content for the user. However, it would be negligent not to discuss the influence trade and consumer publishing has had on e-books in the scholarly and professional disciplines. Huge investments in hardware from technology companies like Sony and Apple, as well as retailers Barnes & Noble and Amazon, have raised the stakes in the game of migrating readers from the printed page to the device screen. Depending on which statistics you choose to believe, these efforts range from moderately successful to significant failures. In the consumer space, "e" delivery has significant value in terms of portability and access. Content can now be delivered wirelessly to proprietary devices such as a Kindle or Nook or rendered in a web browser quickly and conveniently. Major booksellers and publishers report steadily increasing e-book sales to individuals (*Publishers Weekly*, 2011; Kincaid, 2011). The fallout from this transition can already be seen in the demise of Borders Books (Checkler and Trachtenberg, 2011) with many other retailers and members of the supply chain also at risk. Barriers to adoption of e-books in the trade space—clumsy digital rights management (DRM) and platform incompatibility—will be solved over time by the market, and digital delivery of these linear documents, perfectly suited for a monodirectional reading experience, will continue to grow.

Health sciences publishers have enjoyed moderate success in the consumer space to date, but they are limited by the fact that their content, and, more importantly, the manner in which their content is consumed, is uniquely *not* suited for delivery on these "reader-based" devices. One of the largest publishers in scientific and technical publishing recently recalled the majority of their titles from the Amazon Kindle program because of an extraordinarily high amount of customer complaints resulting from unusable content. It seems that EPUB as a "turnkey" format simply cannot handle the tables, formulas, and Greek letters frequently used in professional and scientific texts. An "app," custom-created for a user and a specific set of content, is not and will never be an e-book. For health sciences content in the long term, the cachet of a fancy device will not be able to overcome the limited search capabilities, linear presentation, and poor navigation innate in the e-readers available in the market today. For professional content, "apps" will be the way of the future, and e-readers will be relegated to content and uses more appropriate to their capabilities.

What's Happening Now: Products and Strategies

In the academic world, e-books, approximately five years behind scholarly journals in the migration from print to digital, are in the spotlight now. Libraries are trying to transition their print collection from print to digital, and publishers are trying to deliver their books in "e" through the right channel at the right price, as cost-effectively as possible. Everyone agrees that the printed book is moving to electronic delivery, but for publishers with legacy businesses to support, the challenge is to manage this transition in a manner that ensures that their company will continue to be viable in the new digital world. The line between protecting a lagging textbook line and hindering innovation that could serve them well in the future is sometimes hard to discern. They are also trying to figure out how to evolve their traditional book processes to create content and new products that are valued by their customers and delivered electronically.

Can *Harrison's Principles of Internal Medicine* evolve into a knowledge base that can compete with a born digital product like *UpToDate*? How much will this cost to develop? Do we have the skill set to do it? The infrastructure? How quickly can it be done? All of these questions demand answers and are the focus of most medical publishers today.

Most publishers are developing proprietary "e" strategies based on their book content ranging from web-delivered PDF to fully featured applications that extend the value of the content. In addition to proprietary strategies, most publishers have some sort of relationship with aggregators or third parties to distribute their content to various classes of customers.

Unlike the past, this strategy will be less one-dimensional and more like groups or bundles of strategies bound together in a three-dimensional matrix. Partners in one channel may be competitors in another, and customers may also be competitors. A good example of this is the new University Publishing Online (http://ebooks.cambridge.org/upo/) from Cambridge University Press. This distribution platform, built by a publisher, is designed to aggregate content not only from Cambridge but also from other university presses in a single web interface and is a welcome option for university presses struggling with the migration to "e." Formerly simple, discrete sales channels have morphed into complex ecosystems.

Currently, the trends in professional e-books seem to be favoring individual titles versus collections, allowing libraries in budget-challenged times to select only those titles that they need and measure true return on investment per title via cost per use metrics. The days of the "Big Deal" appear to be at an end, with the exception being large academic research libraries. Additionally, demand or patron-driven access is gaining momentum as a component of acquisitions and can afford libraries the chance to involve their users in helping build and manage their collections. These trends can prove daunting for publishers and other content providers, much more accustomed to selling their information in a just-in-case environment, but it will force content providers to focus on their core competency: producing the best content and putting a plan in place to maximize its use.

> Given the complexity of the market and the increased need to innovate, financial and otherwise, there is a large amount of pressure to decide and decide correctly on a strategy that maximizes revenue and disseminates content to as wide an audience as possible.

The Nature of Change

The human mind is conditioned to expect change to happen quickly. The phenomenon of the "overnight success" is well engrained in our collective psyche and romanticized in popular culture. The reality of change is much less dynamic and much more iterative, and so it is with the shift from print to digital. We are in an era of change unseen since the move from an agrarian economy to the industrial economy; we are transitioning from an industrial to a knowledge-based economy. In publishing and information media, this change has been emergent since the advent of the computer in the 1960s and continues today with the move from the printed page in books to digital ink on screen. It is always somewhat amusing to hear technology experts declare the "death" of the book. More accurately they are referring to the death of the printed page as the sole means of communicating secondary source content.

Whether this information is delivered on a page, on a desktop, or via a tablet is not the essence of what content creation and publishing is about. Publishers who see e-books as just one more channel through which to deliver information to any relevant user will continue to define strategies to do just that. Until the next big thing comes along.

References

Checkler, Joseph, and Jeffrey A. Trachtenberg. 2011. "Borders Begins a New Chapter...11." *Wall Street Journal*, February 17. http://online.wsj.com/article/SB10001424052748703373404576147922340434998.html.

Fialkoff, Francine. 2011. "ALA Midwinter 2011: ProQuest Acquires ebrary in Pre-ALA Announcement." *Library Journal*, January 6. http://www.libraryjournal.com/lj/home/888682-264/ala_midwinter_2011_proquest_acquires.html.csp.

Hadro, Josh. 2011. "HarperCollins Puts 26 Loan Cap on EBook Circulations." *Library Journal*, February 25. http://www.libraryjournal.com/lj/home/889452-264/harpercollins_puts_26_loan_cap.html.csp.

Kincaid, Jason. 2011. "That Was Fast: Amazon's Kindle Sales Outpace Print (It Only Took 4 Years)." *Tech Crunch*, May 19. http://techcrunch.com/2011/05/19/that-was-fast-amazons-kindle-ebook-sales-surpass-print-it-only-took-four-years/.

McEvoy, Kathleen. 2010. "EBSCO Publishing to Acquire NetLibrary Division from OCLC." *PR Web*, March 17. http://www.prweb.com/releases/EBSCOPublishing/OCLC/prweb3739054.htm.

Owen, Laura Hazard. 2011. "Authors Guild: Kindle Owners' Lending Library Is 'Nonsense.'" paidContent.org, November 11. http://paidcontent.org/article/419-authors-guild-kindle-owners-lending-library-is-nonsense/.

Publishers Weekly. 2011. "E-Book Sales Up 159% in Quarter, Print Falls." *Publishers Weekly*, May 19. http://www.publishersweekly.com/pw/by-topic/industry-news/financial-reporting/article/47343-e-book-sales-up-159-in-quarter-print-falls.html.

United Press International. 1990. "Dutch Firm to Buy Lippincott for $250 Million." *Los Angeles Times*, May 22. http://articles.latimes.com/1990-05-22/business/fi-294_1_j-b-lippincott.

Wolters Kluwer, 2011. "Wolters Kluwer Health 2011 Point of Care Survey." Wolters Kluwer. Accessed November 21. http://www.wolterskluwerhealth.com/News/Documents/White%20Papers/Wolters%20Kluwer%20Health%20Survey%20Executive%20Summary-Media.pdf.

E-Book Publishing— The View from the Library

Nadia J. Lalla

Introduction

The previous chapter discussed the role of the publishing industry in the evolution of e-books, including economic and technological drivers, the changing character and dynamics of customer relationships, differing calculations of price points and costs, and the unforeseen and sometimes undesired consequences of these transformations to publishers. This chapter looks at many of the same issues through the lenses of e-book publishing models and trends and their impact on libraries.

Some Background Information

As soon as the decision is made to purchase books in digital format for a library, a myriad of decisions must be made. Should e-books be purchased via a single exclusive publisher or a third-party vendor? What format will the e-book have? On which e-book platform will it appear? How should libraries acquire e-books? The answers to these questions can unexpectedly shape a library's collections and its future decisions regarding the funding of those collections.

A publisher's e-book offerings are primarily for frontlist titles from their imprints; however, backlist titles are increasingly available as publishers recognize that libraries are especially interested in obtaining this older content. In addition, as more content is born-digital, these future backlist titles will always be available in electronic form unlike their current print counterparts. In contrast, a third-party vendor can offer newer e-books from a variety of publishers, but fewer backlist titles are likely to be found.

E-books can exist in a variety of electronic formats. The most popular format is the PDF, or Portable Document Format (Vasileiou, Hartley, and Rowley, 2009), followed by Extensible Hypertext Markup Language (XHTML)–enhanced files with hotlinks that permit easy movement within the e-book and seamless navigation between e-books on the same platform. Additional formats include Exchange Data Format (EDF) and

Electronic Publishing (EPUB). All of these variations can occur within a single publisher or with the same e-book title. Publishers may even offer the same e-book on different e-book platforms. Elsevier is an example of a publisher/vendor with multiple proprietary e-book platforms and whose e-books are available in multiple formats on third-party platforms. The seventh edition of *Miller's Anesthesia* is published by Churchill Livingstone, an imprint of Elsevier. It is available as an e-book on Elsevier's MD Consult e-book platform but not on its ScienceDirect platform. This e-book can be accessed and read on a handheld device using the MD Consult Mobile website. The same e-book can be purchased for Amazon's Kindle e-book reader. It can also be read on an iPad using the Kindle e-book reader app. The result? The same content but a very different user experience on each platform and device.

Unlike print books, which generally have the same shape and method of use, each e-book platform is intentionally unique. From the library perspective, this can lead to confusion and frustration for patrons as they navigate the idiosyncrasies of each interface whether on a personal computer or a handheld device. For example, the location of navigational buttons is different on each platform, and printing options can be extremely restricted with one publisher and limitless with another. This "versatility" can drive librarians to select preferred e-book platforms as a means of standardizing e-book offerings for patrons. However, an unintended consequence is that the library's e-books are then limited to items that are available only on those platforms. This can exclude popular bestsellers that are published on other e-book platforms. In addition, when publishers such as McGraw-Hill choose to restrict their content to their proprietary platforms, librarians with restricted acquisitions funds are forced to make difficult and exclusionary choices.

Librarians are looking to the publishing industry to provide the electronic equivalent of the physical book which can be used universally by anyone. To some extent, librarians are pained witnesses to the fractured e-book landscape as they watch publishers attempt to control the distribution and presentation of their e-content. It is not possible for all e-book providers to survive. The industry has already seen the demise of one major publishing distributor with the bankruptcy of Borders. Who and what will be left? The entire e-publishing industry is in a state of transition. The net effect is ongoing anxiety in libraries as they try to correctly guess what the possible outcomes are. As outlined later, e-book collections are bottomless financial black holes. Libraries could potentially sink tens of thousands of dollars into e-books with a particular publisher or aggregator platform and have nothing to show for this investment if they have backed the wrong choice.

Purchase versus Subscription E-Book Models

Publishers and third-party aggregators provide e-books to libraries using a purchase model, a subscription model, or a combination of both. The primary difference between a purchase model and a subscription model is ownership of the e-content. E-book subscriptions are comparable to serial subscriptions. Annual rates can be influenced by the number of concurrent or potential users, the number and location of access sites, and the subject content or genre of the e-book. However, unlike a print serial, at the end of the subscription period the library does not own the e-book. This is a model that is increasingly popular for many public, academic, and special libraries.

Cost Considerations

Traditionally, libraries purchase materials for their collections. However, in the current austere economic climate, subscription models for e-books have become an attractive solution. The advantage of this model is that typically subscription rates for an individual e-book are substantially less than the purchase price of the same e-book. For libraries that are unable to absorb wild swings in acquisition costs, a flat-fee subscription rate with a prescribed annual increase that provides desired content may be worth the additional short-term costs. Purchase of e-book content may be the ideal response to spend one-time funds that "expire" at the end of a fiscal year. While a subscription may initially be less costly than the purchase price, the annual costs cumulated over the life of the edition will usually make this the more expensive option. Libraries will need to analyze their budgets in both short and long terms. More discussion of the cost considerations can be found in Chapter 5, "Selecting E-Books," and Chapter 7, "Budgeting for E-Books." Additional costs can include annual access or maintenance fees, fees to obtain cataloging records, fees for obtaining purchased content on media, and the hidden staff costs of catalog maintenance and troubleshooting of digital resources. While many of these costs are also associated with the processing of print resources, it is important to consider when examining all budget factors, including personnel and processing.

> ### "ADDED" COSTS OF E-BOOKS
>
> - Annual access or maintenance fees
> - Fees for catalog records
> - Fees for archival media
> - Staff time for catalog maintenance
> - Staff time to troubleshoot access issues
> - Staff time to instruct patrons on use of e-book platforms or how to download to e-book readers or mobile devices

Collection Sustainability: Perpetual Access versus Nonperpetual Access E-Book Models

In a perpetual access e-book model, the library agrees to purchase e-books from a publisher or aggregator. Wiley, Elsevier, EBSCO, and Coutts are some of the publishers and aggregators that offer these types of purchase models. These e-books can be accessed on a publisher- or vendor-supplied platform, or the purchasing library can choose to mount the e-books on local servers. Generally the publisher or aggregator also agrees to provide the library with a digital copy of the purchased content. Libraries can download the data remotely, or the data may be supplied via CDs or DVDs. These data dumps may come with or without data field tags and associated images, but they cannot be converted to something usable without additional programming and coding. There may be costs associated with obtaining these digital copies of e-books. These copies also need to be stored securely and checked regularly for data degradation.

This requires potential investments of server space, storage media, and staff time. A complicating factor is that some publishers specify that these digital copies will become available only *if* the company dissolves. This puts libraries in the unenviable position of hoping that they will be able to retrieve their purchased content before the company disappears.

In a nonperpetual access model, purchased or subscribed e-books are accessible only via the publisher or vendor that provides the content and platform interface. If the publishing company dissolves or is acquired by another company, access is not guaranteed. Vendor or publishing agreements do not necessarily transfer intact to the new company.

Is perpetual access important or relevant to all libraries? The answer will vary depending on the type of library, the audience it serves, the mission of its parent institution (where appropriate), and the library's ability or desire to manage electronic content. Is the library or the parent institution willing to relinquish ownership of resources as part of its identity? Academic libraries in particular have been reluctant to move to a nonperpetual access model because of the longer term impact on historical collections. Some libraries choose to have a hybrid model where only one copy of a print book is purchased and additional copies are leased as e-books. As demand for the latest Sue Grafton novel diminishes, the purchased copy is retained in the permanent collection and the e-copies are cancelled. Such strategies allow libraries to respond quickly and with flexibility to local needs.

There are other issues of usability of perpetual access content. Several years ago, Gale discovered that, while it owned the text of an e-book, it did not own the rights to the images. Because the e-book was an encyclopedia of animals, the images were crucial to the usability of the book. Unfortunately, this was determined only when the library that purchased the e-book examined the CD that contained the perpetual access content (Scott Dennis, University of Michigan, October 2005, personal communication). In a more recent example, Amazon's decision to remove content from its Kindle e-readers rankled many users and prompted a lawsuit (Claburn, 2009).

It sometimes appears as if publishers themselves are not sure how to approach the business of selling their electronic content to libraries. While concerns over ownership of copyrights continue to be of paramount importance to publishers, pricing models for e-books (and, in general, most e-resources) are not consistent throughout the industry. As a result, the pendulum can swing widely from e-books that cost $9.99 to purchase and download onto an e-reader to an e-textbook that can cost $3,000 a year for an institutional site license subscription. It is difficult to know what a "reasonable" price should be for an e-book, and there are no industry guidelines to use.

Multiple Formats of the Same Content

Librarians are grappling with the demand to offer the same book across a variety of formats. Student A wants a hard copy of *Othello*. Student B wants to use an e-book version so he can highlight textual passages, add marginalia, and use it in an exam situation. The notes will be saved forever and are linked to his personalized user account. Student C just needs the text of the play long enough to pass the mandatory English class; an e-book that he doesn't have to buy is ideal. Student D wants a portable version that she can read on her iPad. Publishers are aware of these differing needs and are catering their products accordingly. The result is that a library can easily obtain an e-book that is a duplicate copy of something that is already owned in print.

How should this new content be presented to the library patron? Is it better to use a single record where multiple formats for *Othello* are displayed in a single screen? Is it sufficient to load records for each format into the online public access catalog (OPAC) and use icons to distinguish between e-books and print books? Who provides those records? If it's the publisher, how complete is the cataloging? How easy (or difficult) is it to integrate these records into the OPAC? Would patrons rather just go to the e-book platform and browse?

Many publishers will provide catalog records to download, import, or integrate into the OPAC. There may be a cost for obtaining the catalog records. Note that "obtain" is a catchall for where the catalog record may be. Some publishers (e.g., Elsevier) provide MARC records on a remote site; the onus is on the library to retrieve those records. Other publishers send records to a third-party vendor. Some libraries use a vendor such as Serials Solutions that obtains the records from publishers and ensures that these records meet a particular standard before sending them on to a library. Alternatively, it may be less expensive to create a record depending on the depth of cataloging desired. The publisher-supplied record may not meet the library's standards for record importation.

Impact on Collection Sustainability

Are duplicate copies of material in different formats important to a library's users? For many public libraries, having the same book available as an e-book and as a print copy fits their multigenerational user population. For those libraries that have storage issues (reduced physical footprint, remote storage, damaged buildings), having an e-book of an already owned print book may satisfy patron demand with minimal impact on a library's physical facilities. This is of greater importance as libraries undertake regional or local print retention projects, weed physical collections, or renovate spaces.

The problem with having an item in multiple formats is that the library pays for the same book several times over. While some publishers choose to offer e-books only through their proprietary platform, other publishers will make their e-content available to as many vendors as possible, including aggregators. In disciplines such as medicine, an e-book may be 1.5 to 2 times (Stielstra, 2011) the cost of its print counterpart and is often not released simultaneously with the print publication. This is a regular discussion topic on the Medical Library Association's (MLA) MEDLIB-L and the MLA Collection Development Section's

MLA-CDS e-mail electronic discussion lists. In this subject area, the demand by clinicians for immediate point-of-need e-books needs to be balanced against a student's long-term use of the same material for coursework.

Another concern when the library offers the same e-book on multiple platforms (e.g., NetLibrary and ebrary and Ovid) is that each vendor has its own restrictions on downloading, printing, concurrent users, "active" time in the book, etc. This can be extremely confusing and frustrating for patrons. They can see that an interface is different, but they don't know that they can print only up to ten pages in interface A. If they had selected interface B, they could print the entire chapter. A further discussion of e-book platforms can be found in Chapters 5 and 6.

The "Big Deal" E-Book Package Model

The concept of the Big Deal package has been around for nearly a decade. Initially, these "deals" were bundles of e-journals from a single publisher that contained must-have, highly valued titles and smaller, rarely used journals. It was initially offered as a convenient method by publishers for libraries to receive lots of journal subscriptions at a reduced cost rather than individual title subscriptions. Think of it as bulk buying. These deals tended to be multiyear agreements with a predetermined rate increase from one year to the next. During the contract period, the library usually agreed not to cancel any titles, and publishers could choose to include new or newly acquired titles at little to no extra cost. Pricing could be based on historical spending (usually print subscriptions to which the institution already subscribed), FTE (full-time equivalent) students, population, the number of multisite access points, or any combination thereof. Big Deals were most attractive to academic institutions, larger public libraries, and consortia (e.g., Committee on Institutional Cooperation).

Today, publishers and third-party vendors now offer Big Deal e-book packages. The concept is essentially the same: purchase or subscribe to a large number of e-books for a relatively low cost per item price. Contract periods range from a single year to multiple years. Purchased material is owned outright by the library; subscribed material is leased and remains the property of the publisher or vendor once the contract ends. From the library's perspective, there are advantages and disadvantages to each option (see sidebar, p. 29).

Cost Considerations

The biggest stumbling blocks for librarians who are considering Big Deal e-book packages are the costs, whether subscription or purchase. Many publishers will offer discounts for e-book packages as an incentive; however, these discounts are rarely less expensive than purchasing the print monograph. In some disciplines, for example, science, technology, and medicine (STM), e-book prices are sometimes as much as 1.5 to 2

BIG DEAL PACKAGES: PROS AND CONS

Big Deal E-Book Purchase?

Advantages
- Usually latest e-books (i.e., past 1–3 years of publisher imprints)
- Lots of titles in many subjects
- Usage statistics
- One-time cost for purchase
- Own e-books at end of contract

Disadvantages
- All or nothing
- Lots of titles in many subjects, including those with little or no relevance to the library's constituents
- Large one-time cost up front for purchase that may have a negative impact on the library's overall collection budget
- Ongoing access fees to use publisher platform during and after contract period
- Own e-books at end of contract but don't have infrastructure to mount e-books

Big Deal E-Book Subscription?

Advantages
- Usually latest e-books (i.e., past 1–3 years of publisher imprints)
- Lots of titles in many subjects
- Usage statistics
- Lower subscription cost than purchase cost
- Access to greater number of books than can be purchased
- Don't own e-books at the end of the contract, which may dovetail with a library's space needs or changing readership demands

Disadvantages
- All or nothing
- Lots of titles in many subjects, including those with little or no relevance to the library's constituents
- Don't own e-books at the end of the contract, which may be a problem for libraries where ownership is crucial and necessary

times the cost of the printed book (Newman, 2010). In the case of subscription options, libraries are committing to multiyear agreements in which they guarantee to pay a specified amount annually and cannot cancel. This can be injurious if a library is faced with a drastic reduction in available resource funds.

In addition to the up-front purchase or leasing costs, publishers often require access fees for using their interface. These may be waived at the publisher's discretion or as part of the negotiation process. Depending on how a consortium chooses to distribute the costs of a Big Deal package, libraries with fewer funds can benefit from pooled subscriptions or purchases. In such an agreement, the entire package may be available to all participants regardless of the funds paid.

Unintended costs can occur if a library purchases a Big Deal package and then chooses to discontinue using the publisher's or vendor's native interface. While the library owns the content, it may not have the means (programming time, server space) to mount the content on its own.

Impact on Collection Sustainability

A Big Deal provides maximum bang for the buck. It can be an acceptable solution for a library to quickly provide access to a large number of e-books at reasonable costs if ownership is not an issue. However, it's worthwhile to carefully review the titles offered in a Big Deal:

- Not all titles may be relevant to the library.
- Titles from vanity publishers or less-preferred publishers may be included.
- Even within a single publisher, the quality of one title as compared to another can vary.

The Big Deal packages are not the right fit for every library. If the library has a historical research focus, such as at the larger university libraries, it may be more important to have perpetual access to e-books than to subscribe to collections. Alternatively, different disciplines may require different strategies. A major hospital library may decide that it's more important to subscribe to the latest editions of selected clinical e-textbooks from STAT!Ref than to purchase each edition from Rittenhouse. The hospital library wants to be sure that the latest edition is always available and is not interested in retaining earlier editions.

The Patron-Driven Acquisition (PDA) E-Book Model

In this model, librarians preselect a list of e-book titles and load publisher- or vendor-supplied records into the OPAC. After a predetermined number of views or browses, the library "buys" that content. There are many ways to control what is actually purchased. Limits can be placed on the amount that can be spent at one time, for example, anything that costs more than $50 must be approved by a librarian. To ensure that the request is genuine, access may be restricted to recognized patrons. All requests for purchase can be reviewed prior to purchase. This model takes advantage of crowdsourcing to determine the shape of the collection. It can lead to a user-tailored collection. This may or may not be important depending on what the library's priorities are. PDA can also lead to some unintentional focused purchasing. If a communications class is studying reality TV and its impact on society, the library could potentially buy a lot of e-books on this topic. This does require a shift in thinking about collection development from a just-in-case collection to a just-in-time collection. With this model, librarians can be sure that these titles are desired by patrons and are likely to be circulated.

Librarians should not rely on PDA as the sole means for building collections. PDA is not an effective tool for comprehensive additions and needs to be supplemented. However, these e-books can expediently place content in the hands of patrons when it is needed. Further discussion of using PDA as a selection option can be found in Chapter 5.

Trend: Digital Rights Management (DRM)

The arena of DRM has become increasingly murkier as the legal system, publishers, and libraries have attempted to navigate this unexplored landscape and set beacons at crucial junctures. The protracted Google Book Settlement (http://www.googlebooksettlement.com/) has left all parties unsure about their legal rights. Meanwhile there is ongoing advocacy for authors to retain their copyrights in an era of Open Access publishing solutions, institutional repositories, and mandatory free access to articles published as a result of studies funded by the National Institutes of Health (http://publicaccess.nih.gov/policy.htm). The HathiTrust Digital Library (http://www.hathitrust.org/) recently waded into these discussions by announcing that it would proactively be opening up its orphan works to global Internet access (Quint, 2011). The reaction from the publishing community was swift and preemptive. In September 2011, the Authors Guild filed a lawsuit against HathiTrust in which it claimed that the digital repository was infringing on copyright holders' rights (Authors Guild, 2011).

The immediate impact of DRM events for libraries has been beneficial. While many publishers chose not to participate in Google's mass digitization project, it did galvanize publisher development of e-book options for libraries. The result has been increasingly sophisticated platform interfaces, open dialogues regarding content of interest to libraries, and, most importantly, the availability of e-books. With the HathiTrust Digital Library, thousands of public domain books that were previously inaccessible to most people are now a few mouse clicks away. Meanwhile, Springer-Verlag provides DRM-free e-books for institutional purchase.

Heightened awareness of digital rights has inevitably led to discussions about fair use and interlibrary loan use of e-books. For many publishers and libraries, this is uneasy territory. Libraries are engaged in interlibrary lending operations. Publishers are concerned about losing digital content. For many publishers and libraries, the compromise solution is one that is applied to many electronic journals subscriptions: the lending library may download an article, print the article, and send it via snail mail to the requesting library where it is received, rescanned, and sent to the patron requestor. Publishers are encouraged to include licensing language that includes e-mailing content directly to the requesting library. Residual discussions about copyright fees continue to guide these forays.

Libraries have begun to play with the concept of sharing e-books. OverDrive has partnered with Amazon to offer libraries the option of lending Amazon's e-books using Kindles (OverDrive, 2011). It's too soon to tell if this is a fad or the next big thing. While e-readers remain popular, many people want to carry a single mobile device that has multiple functions: phone, personal organizer, e-mail, social networking, movies, and e-book reader. Publishers are adapting to this need by making content available, but the DRM hasn't caught up yet.

Trend: E-Textbooks

What is the difference between an e-book and an e-book used as an e-textbook? Cost and access. In the science, technology, and medicine (STM) field, textbook purchases by the library are the most requested item. In a print environment, this has meant multiple copies of expensive textbooks on reserve. In the electronic environment, libraries often discover that the e-book version that is available for a student to purchase is not the same version that a library can buy. In many instances, the library cannot purchase an electronic copy at all. Why not? There is a valid concern among publishers that library purchase of an e-textbook means fewer purchases by students or other individuals. When libraries are able to purchase an e-textbook, the accompanying supplementary e-content, such as review questions, practice exams, or lab videos, are unavailable or are restricted to one-time use with an unlock code. At the same time, the cost for the library to acquire an e-textbook can be significantly higher than for a student to buy the same e-textbook.

Beginning in 2011, Amazon began to offer the option of renting e-textbooks using their proprietary e-book reader or e-book mobile app. The Kindle Textbook Rental program lets the customer rent for as long as needed (30 days minimum). The e-book software permits book-marking, highlighting, and note-taking. It's too soon to know if this is a successful business venture. Could this be expanded to libraries, and would more publishers be willing to get involved?

The Future of E-Book Publishing and Libraries: Economic Realities + Emerging Technologies + Cultural Shift

E-books are no longer available exclusively to libraries; publishers are choosing to market directly to the consumer aka the library patron aka the college student aka the small-town lawyer. E-books are advertised in mainstream magazines, on websites, and on television shows. They are transitioning from being the newest thing to being a part of daily life and are no longer the exclusive domain of libraries.

The current recession is characterized by contracting employment opportunities, declining revenues, deflated housing markets, and rising energy prices. For key stakeholders (i.e., the ones providing the money), libraries are increasingly viewed solely as consumers of funding with little or no revenue-generating capacity: perceived equivalent resources and services are freely available via the Internet or should be available only to those who want to pay for them (e.g., Kindles and iPads for e-books, NetFlix for video content, or a *New York Times* personal subscription). The conversation about the impact of e-books in libraries changes significantly when emerging technologies are added to this volatile economic climate. Today, a James Patterson novel is available for purchase on

Amazon.com as a hardcover book, a paperback, an audiobook on CD that can be uploaded to an iPod or smartphone, and an e-book that can be used on various e-book readers. (Amazon even offers the e-book version cheaper than many of its used paperbacks.) As the reading device technology has expanded, the options for reading e-books available to the general public have also expanded (e.g., the Kindle cloud reader, HathiTrust, EPUB formats). Because within-copyright e-books are no longer the exclusive domain of libraries, publishers are choosing to market directly to the consumer. None of the above options requires a *library* to serve as the intermediary.

Parallel developments in emerging social technologies such as Foursquare, Facebook, Google+, and augmented reality will also have an impact on library e-book use. These technologies provide users with new ways in which to interact with books. Imagine Jane Austen's novel *Pride and Prejudice* as an augmented reality e-book. In the scene in which Elizabeth Bennet visits the Pemberley estate and wanders through Darcy's great mansion, the e-book could contain active links that show a 3-D floor map of the house, a biographical sketch of the portraits on the hall, an image of an individual item on an end table including a description of its use, and definitions of words unfamiliar to a twenty-first-century reader. This augmented reality e-book would function much as a current annotated book does. When Foursquare is added, the reader could see who else has visited the fictional Pemberley. With Google+ and Facebook, favorite quotations from the text can be easily shared with friends. Thus reading becomes a social, shared experience. There are many opportunities for the library to be present in such an experience, but this assumes that the library is already present in the user's environment, that funding exists to pursue those opportunities, and that issues of digital and access rights have been addressed.

What does this mean for the e-publishing industry from the library's perspective? Today's libraries and publishers are increasingly engaged in a hostile environment borne of decreasing funds, cultural shifts, and emerging technologies. When both parties work together to create solutions, valued content is presented in a dynamic and engaging manner. Springer's ongoing relationship with the Committee on Institutional Cooperation (CIC) is an example of this. This partnership led to the implementation of MyCopy, an inexpensive print-on-demand service for Springer e-books held in CIC libraries. When publishers and libraries are unable to overcome the obstacles of finances, miscommunication, isolated product development, or technology mismatches, the resultant relationship is strained and can have far-reaching negative consequences. The goal of the 2004 Google Library Project was to digitize every book owned by five prominent libraries. However, a dispute over copyright ownership by authors and publishers led to a protracted and still unresolved legal battle (as of this writing) with Google. Meanwhile, libraries and archives have engaged in other mass digitization projects without the direct support of publishers (e.g., PALINET, the Internet Archive), and publishers have digitized their journal backfiles and book backlists that they sell to libraries which already own print equivalents.

As libraries and publishers look toward the future, it becomes increasingly necessary to acknowledge the symbiotic relationship that exists between the two. Most libraries cannot afford to devote resources, staff, or funding to develop e-book platforms. They also do not own the copyright for the most desired e-books. At the same time, publishers need to sell a defined amount of product to libraries. Very few medical students want to buy a $2,000 e-book on anatomy; they rarely want to spend the $150 for the required print anatomy textbook. To whom do publishers expect to sell this content? For both parties, cost is a major factor in the decision to purchase or produce e-book content. The next few years will be tumultuous throughout the e-book publishing world as libraries, publishers, and patrons/customers determine the future developments of e-books.

References

Authors Guild. 2011. "Authors Guild, Australian Society of Authors, Quebec Writers Union Sue Five U.S. Universities." Authors Guild, September 12. http://www.authorsguild.org/advocacy/articles/authors-3.html.

Claburn, Thomas. 2009. "Amazon Settles Kindle Deletion Lawsuit for $150,000." *Information Week*, October 2. http://www.informationweek.com/news/internet/ebusiness/220300915.

Newman, Michael L. 2010. "Collections Strategies for Electronic Books." *Information Outlook* 14, no. 4: 10–12.

OverDrive. 2011. "OverDrive and Amazon Launch Kindle(r) Compatibility with Library eBooks." OverDrive, September 21. http://overdrive.com/News/OverDrive-and-Amazon-launch-Kindle-compatibility-with-Library-eBooks.

Quint, Barbara. 2011. "University of Michigan Libraries Target HathiTrust's Orphan Works." *Information Today*, June 6. http://newsbreaks.infotoday.com/NewsBreaks/University-of-Michigan-Libraries-Target-HathiTrusts-Orphan-Works-75863.asp.

Stielstra, Julie. 2011. "CHAT: Still Struggling with E-Books." *MEDLIB-L* (listserv), July 20. http://list.uvm.edu/cgi-bin/wa?A2=ind1107c&L=MEDLIB-L&D=0&P=74639.

Vasileiou, Magdalini, Richard Hartley, and Jennifer Rowley. 2009. "An Overview of the E-Book Marketplace." *Online Information Review* 33, no. 1: 173–192.

E-Books in Detail

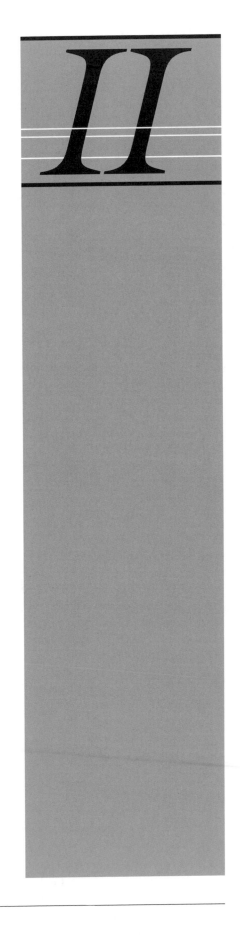

E-Books in Public Libraries

Rebecca Felkner

Introduction

E-books have been available for public library use since the late 1990s, but only recently have public library patrons shown more than a scant interest in them. It has taken more than ten years for e-books to attract interest due to factors such as a lack of availability of popular fiction and nonfiction titles in the early years, lack of portability until the better designed e-readers arrived on the scene in the late 2000s, restrictive digital rights management, and proprietary hardware and software. This chapter addresses the use of e-books in public libraries, including starting an e-book collection, staffing and budgeting needs, and best practices.

In 2010, e-book usage exploded in public libraries. Suddenly e-book usage statistics were increasing by tens and hundreds of percentages instead of a small trickle of increase as was seen for the previous years. According to Schiller (2011: 10), "2010 was a landmark year for the e-book industry." The author backs up this claim with the facts that in July 2010 Amazon announced that for the first time it was selling more e-books than print books, that the Association of American Publishers and the International Digital Publishing Forum announced a 250 percent increase in e-book sales for the third quarter of 2010 compared to the same time frame in 2009, and that the *New York Times* announced it would start publishing weekly e-book bestseller lists.

The soaring popularity of e-books can perhaps best be explained by two reasons: the portable e-reader technology has greatly improved, and the reading public has become familiar enough with the technology, smartphones, and other mobile devices to want to use it. The e-book industry is experiencing what the audiobook industry experienced at the advent of digitized content availability. Burkey (2011: 62) writes: "As the print publishing world deals with the shift to digital e-books, the audiobook community responds 'been there, done that.'" Downloadable audiobooks were much more successful when digitized content became available, because they were able to be downloaded and played on already popular portable devices that were also used to listen to downloadable music. Patrons were already familiar and comfortable with the listening device technologies. E-readers needed a similar length of time to be designed, upgraded, and changed enough until they became a tool that the general public could feel comfortable with. In a May 2010 article about the use of e-books in public libraries, Duncan (2010: 44) states that "improving technology and increased availability of content have led to many of the constraints of this area of the market falling away." Once the general public started to become comfortable with e-readers, more companies started to design, upgrade, and market their own versions, and more retail stores started selling them. These developments showed that "improving technology, decreasing costs of devices, and improving content will further drive uptake of both devices and e-resources" (Duncan, 2010: 52).

Start Your E-Book Collection

Starting and building an e-book collection takes forethought. You will need to do a bit of research into the digital needs and wants of your library and your community:

- Gauge your patrons' needs.
- Choose formats.
- Select lending methods.
- Select the genres.

Gauge Your Patrons' Needs

Do not go blindly into offering an e-book collection to your public library patrons. Is this a service that your library's community wants and needs? Gauge your patrons' thoughts of such a collection by any way that will work with your community: conduct a survey, keep track of requests for e-books, ask your public services staff what patrons are saying to them about e-books, assess the technology IQ and capabilities of your community, talk to neighboring libraries, and weigh the idea of "if you build it, they will come." If it is too early to introduce e-books to your patrons, reexamine the idea every few months.

Choose Formats

Once you decide to offer an e-collection to your library's patrons, determine what formats (e-books, downloadable audiobooks, e-video, and e-music) you will purchase and what percentage of each of these formats. This decision could be guided by your library's existing collection development policy, by analyzing your library's current usage statistics, by asking for patron feedback about what formats would be used most, and by information gained from library literature or anecdotal information from colleagues.

Before choosing an e-vendor for your library, determine what publishers a vendor works with, what offerings that vendor has available in each format, and what download methods are available. For instance, if the community your library serves does not have a high percentage of homes with broadband connectivity, your patrons will encounter very slow download times for the e-book files. You can look up your community's level of broadband connectivity and related information at the website National Broadband Map (http://www.broadbandmap.gov/), a collaboration of the National Telecommunications and Information Administration and the Federal Communications Commission. If your community does not rank high in broadband access, it will be important for the e-book vendor to offer the ability to download e-items in pieces such as by chapter or section instead of an entire book when downloading books or by song instead of an entire CD when downloading music. Also, check with your e-book vendors to determine if they permit libraries to allow patrons to download e-books and audiobooks on the shared public computers at libraries. If this is allowed, let your patrons know they can bring their devices to the library to download e-materials.

Select Lending Methods

Once you make the decision to offer e-books to your patrons, decide how that will be accomplished. You can lend e-books solely as an online offering, or you may decide to lend e-readers to your patrons, or you may do both. Lending e-books online will allow patrons with a valid library card from your library to check out and download e-books at any time of the day or night from anywhere they have a computer or e-reader with Internet service. Lending e-readers will allow patrons who don't have an e-reader or a computer to borrow and use e-books. While offering e-books online for patrons to download to their own devices is an accepted practice, the legality of lending e-readers is not black and white. Amazon and Apple both have terminology in their license agreements that software and devices are for personal use only and/or that lending is prohibited (Hirtle, 2010). Amazon has also issued statements that their terms of service prohibit libraries from lending Kindles, but Amazon also declines to enforce those terms of service and Amazon staffers give conflicting answers when asked if lending Kindles is allowed (Oder, 2009). That said, a simple web search reveals that numerous public libraries are lending e-readers to patrons.

If you do lend e-readers, your library may choose to lend e-readers with no books on them, preload the e-readers with permanent titles, or load the e-readers with books that the patron requests. If you lend blank e-readers, patrons will be able to download titles of their choosing to the e-readers. When a patron returns the e-reader, your library would then wipe any e-books from the e-reader to prepare to lend it as a blank e-reader again. When lending a preloaded e-reader, you can download a number of titles to each e-reader permanently. You may want to download titles based on a different theme (mystery, romance, westerns, finance, bestsellers, etc.) to each of the e-readers so that patrons can check out an e-reader with a particular genre of books already loaded.

Select the Genres

What genres will you purchase for your e-book collection? Your decision may be guided by your existing collection development policy and usage statistics. Keep in mind that patrons who use e-books may have different interests and may use the e-collection differently than your library's hard copy collection. You may find that your patrons like to use only popular reading materials from your e-book collection instead of books that are more reference oriented, or you may find just the opposite. In other words, you need to analyze the needs of your users, which may vary by library or geographic region. In public libraries, e-book collections typically contain mostly popular literature and nonfiction, but some reference titles are available. Check with your vendors to determine if they offer the genres you are looking for. Initially you may examine usage statistics from your library's print collection to guide your e-book purchases. Also search library and publishing literature for information about what genres are most popular in the e-book industry and study your e-book statistics to see your library's e-book usage trends. It may take awhile to see the trends, but keep track of the usage statistics to determine what genres are most popular and you will most likely see trends eventually. Usage trends should also be available from your e-book vendor, which will have information based on its national sales.

Staff Functions

Unless your library joins an e-book purchasing cooperative or is part of a library network that handles all tasks associated with starting and running an e-book collection, adding e-books to your library's collection will create new work for your staff throughout your library. Additional staff positions, such as an electronic resource librarian, may need to be created and/or new responsibilities may be added to existing staff positions. Additional functions may include:

- electronic resource management,
- collection development,
- technical services,
- publicity,
- staff training, and
- patron training.

Electronic Resource Management

You may decide to create an electronic resource librarian position. The electronic resource librarian can be responsible for either coordinating the work of others involved in e-book services or performing all e-services, such as collection development, vendor relations, ordering, technical services, publicity, staff training, and patron training. Adding a new position may be cost prohibitive, yet dividing the work among existing staffers may overload them. In either case, someone on staff needs to coordinate the effort. Work with your staff to determine the best way to handle the work created by having an e-book collection. If you are part of a local or state network and share either an integrated library system or group collections, investigate what level of resource management is available through the consortium.

Collection Development

E-book collection development can be handled by one staff person or divided among several staff as makes sense for your library. The money for the e-books budget can come from one line item, such as an electronic resources line item, or from the line items of the departments where the e-books' subject matter fits. Determine what types of e-books your library will offer (fiction, nonfiction, adult, youth, etc.) and order accordingly. Studying your library's e-book usage statistics can help you make decisions on how much to spend on e-books and on what genres. E-book selection can be done in a variety of ways:

- manually,
- automatically through preset selection plans, or
- pay-per-view purchase plans.

Ask your vendor or vendors what selection options are available.

Manual Collection Development

If you choose the titles manually, you'll keep control of what you purchase, but it will take staff time to manually select individual titles. Staff will need to monitor new title lists and keep abreast of publishing trends in e-books. You can also survey customers to determine what titles they'd like to have available and keep an eye on the holds ratio—the number of holds per title. If the holds ratio gets too high on a particular title, you may want to purchase extra copies.

Automatic Purchase Plan

If your library creates an automatic purchase plan, where books are automatically sent to the library based on a library- or vendor-determined profile, you will save staff time but lose some control of what you purchase. If you do use an automatic purchase plan, you may set up a profile by topic or subject for e-book selection or purchase a vendor-chosen collection of titles. For example, your staff can set up a purchase plan based on a holds ratio, or they can choose to add bestselling titles or titles that become available from predetermined authors, genres, or publishers. Choosing a vendor-chosen collection of titles can be a good, fast way to start an e-book collection if your library has little or no staff to assign to e-book collection development.

Pay-Per-View

If you choose a pay-per-view option, your vendor will give you a list of available e-book titles and your library will purchase a title only if a patron looks at it and/or downloads it. This is also called patron-driven acquisition (PDA), which is discussed in detail in Chapter 5, "Selecting E-Books."

Most public libraries use a combination of manual and automatic purchasing. Choose your collection development method based on what makes most staffing sense for your library. Ask your vendors how they allow libraries to select e-books. If they do offer the automatic purchase plan method or pay-per-view purchasing method, set a spending limit with the vendor to ensure that you do not spend more than your budget allows.

Technical Services

You will need to decide how to provide patrons access to the e-books. Will you link to the e-books from your library's webpage, will you integrate the e-books into your catalog, or will you do both? Your decision may rest on how much money and staff time you have to devote to purchasing MARC records for the e-books and loading them into your catalog and on the staff time and expertise available to link to e-books from your webpage. If you can manage to do both, do so, as more access points means the materials will be easier for your patrons to find. Providing a link or links on your webpage to your e-book collection will require very little added work and little to no cost, whereas integrating the e-books into your catalog will require both technical services work and funds to purchase the MARC records. If purchasing MARC records, your technical services department will need to tweak the MARC records if necessary and input the MARC records into your catalog. Before signing a contract with the e-book vendor, determine the method for obtaining the MARC records—will the vendor supply the MARC records to you, or will the vendor order the MARC records for you, or will your library have to order the MARC records on your own? Include MARC records cost in your e-book budget, and add money to your technical services budget if you will integrate them into your catalog. For more information on budgeting, see Chapter 7; see Chapter 8 for a detailed analysis of cataloging issues and best practices.

Publicity

Make sure to promote your e-book collection to your community. This task could fall to your electronic services librarian, public services staff, or possibly may be best handled by whoever handles publicity for your library. Although the usual publicity methods, such as signs or events in the library and articles in the library newsletter or local paper, will work, also try publicity methods that take advantage of web technologies that allow patrons to connect directly to e-books; for instance, add "staff recommends" e-book lists to your library's webpage and include links directly to those e-books in your collection, or add book jackets of the e-books that will open an excerpt that patrons can read. For more information about publicizing e-books, see the E-Books in Practice section, Example 2, "Marketing E-Books in a Public Library."

Staff Training

E-book technology may be very foreign to your library's staff. Cultivate at least one or two (or more) e-book experts on your staff. Although any staff member could fill this role, many times your reference staff, electronic resource librarian, or your information technology staff will already have the skills to work with e-books and e-readers or will feel comfortable obtaining these skills. If needed, send your library's e-book expert(s) to e-book training (usually supplied by vendors to teach the nuances of a particular platform) and attend conferences, webinars, regional workshops, and continuing education programs sponsored by professional library associations and library technology publishers, such as *Information Today* (http://www.infotoday.com/), which also sponsors the Computers in Libraries annual meeting, or *Library Journal* (http://www.libraryjournal.com/). Nonlibrary-specific organizations may create or sponsor e-book training opportunities also; BookExpo America (http://bookexpoamerica.com/), Digital Book World (http://www.digitalbookworld.com/), and the International Digital Publishing Forum (http://www.idpf.org/) all sponsor or have sponsored e-book conferences or training of some sort. Also consider attending an EDUCAUSE conference (http://www.educause.edu/).

Plan to help your entire staff become at least slightly familiar with the technology so they in turn can answer patrons' basic questions about the e-book collection and e-readers or can point patrons to the staff e-book experts. Offering group or one-on-one staff training is optimal; if neither is possible, provide a training webinar or videos and training handouts with definitions of e-book technology jargon and step-by-step instructions for downloading e-books to computers and several types of e-readers. Your e-book vendor may provide training to your staff, and local home electronics stores may offer to send one of their staffers to train your library staff. If your budget allows, purchase e-readers on which your staff can practice downloading e-books.

Patron Training

Staff will likely need to provide some level of training to patrons on using e-books. This may consist of nothing more than pointing a patron to the e-book collection, or it may entail providing one-on-one training sessions during which a staff member can help a patron with an e-reader device. Group e-book training sessions or web tutorials can also be created by staff to train patrons on using their e-readers with your library's e-book collection. Staff should prepare step-by-step handouts about how to download e-books to home computers and e-readers. The handouts can be distributed to patrons at service desks, can be added to the web tutorials, and can be used for one-on-one or group e-book training sessions. Preparing a handout with downloading instructions for each specific e-reader, or for the most common e-readers, is especially helpful. Most, if not all, e-reader vendors offer how-to-use instructions and online tutorials on their websites that you can use for your own library's patron instruction, and other libraries may allow you to use instructional materials that they have already created. Utilize any of the options to get instructional materials to your patrons.

Set Policies

You will need policies for the different aspects of your e-book collection just as you have policies in place for your materials of other formats. You will:

- determine who makes the policies,
- set e-book circulation policies, and
- set e-reader circulation policies.

Determine Who Makes the Policies

Who will set the policies you put in place regarding your library's e-book collection? Does the decision-making process rest with your administration or board of directors? Do you ask for staff input? Unlike your physical materials collections, some of the policies may be dictated by the e-book vendors you use as they ultimately have control of the files that contain your e-books, and the e-books may have limits and controls encrypted into their files by the publishers. However, your library will have the ability and responsibility to set many of the policies regarding the e-books that you purchase. For more information on negotiating licenses and examining publishers' digital rights policies, read Chapter 6.

Set E-Book Circulation Policies

Setting the length of time a patron can keep an e-book is a decision your vendor may control, though possibly not. For lending periods, a vendor may give a choice of 7, 10, or 14 days, for example, or may allow you to set your own length of time. Your vendor may also offer a feature in the patron interface that allows your patrons to choose the length of time they'd like to borrow the e-book. Length of lending periods may vary for e-books and downloadable audiobooks. Your vendor also may set the number of e-books a patron can check out at one time, although this decision is typically left to the library. Fourteen to 21 days is a typical length of time to set for e-book lending periods, but your library should decide what works best for you taking into consideration the size of your e-book collection versus the patron demand for it. When the question "What is the CIRC (circulation) interval for downloadables at your library?" was asked in a 2009 study of 41 libraries, 43.9 percent reported lending downloadables for 14 days and 46.3 percent reported lending downloadables for 21 days (Genco, 2009).

Because the e-book almost certainly resides on the vendor's or publisher's server, allowing a renewal or the ability to return an e-book early will depend on your vendor's system capability or on the publisher's contractual rules. If the vendor's system allows renewals, you will need to determine if an item can be renewed if there is a hold against the book, and you may be able to decide how long the renewal period will be—the same length as the initial checkout or less time. Early e-book return is a feature that is sometimes available with Adobe PDF and EPUB formats, and sometimes early return can be handled by giving the patron a lending length time choice at checkout. However, publishers' contractual rules may prohibit early return and/or renewals for a variety of reasons. Publishers, as new to the e-book industry as libraries, continue to determine how to allow purchase and use of e-books that will protect their ownership and ability to profit while pricing e-books affordably.

Set E-Reader Circulation Policies

If your library circulates e-readers, you will need to set policies to govern the service and also set policies to protect the e-readers. To govern the service, your library will need to set lending length times, renewal guidelines, and other typical circulation details. To protect the e-readers, your library may also set more restrictive circulation policies for them in the event a patron damages or fails to return them; some examples follow:

- Patrons must be 18 years old.
- Patrons must not owe any fines or have any blocks on their account.
- There are no renewals.
- Patrons must sign an agreement stating they will pay for the item in full if it is damaged or lost.

Some of the e-readers, such as Amazon Kindles, Sony Readers, and Barnes & Noble Nooks, are connected to their respective companies with a password-protected account. Do not give the password to patrons. Doing so will leave you wide open to allowing patrons to purchase e-books on the e-reader. To be extra careful, have your patrons agree in writing not to purchase any e-books using the e-reader's account if they somehow access it.

Circulating preloaded e-readers will allow patrons who want to read e-books but don't own an e-reader the opportunity to use e-books. Your library may want to preload each e-reader with several books from a certain genre or a mix of genres, or your library may circulate blank e-readers and allow patrons to choose what titles to download from your library's e-book collection. If preloading the e-readers with titles, you will want to catalog the individual e-readers and list the titles they hold as added titles or subjects in the MARC record.

Budget/Allocate Funds

In offering e-books to your library's patrons you will incur start-up and ongoing costs. You can shoulder all the costs yourself but it can be very cost-effective for you to join with other libraries into an e-book purchasing cooperative, a regional library network or consortium.

Start-Up Costs

Start-up costs may be incurred for:

- creating an e-book website,
- integrating the titles into your library's online catalog,
- setting up the account with an e-book vendor,
- purchasing the initial collection, and
- purchasing the e-readers, if providing this service.

Start-up costs can depend on the vendor you work with. Creating an e-book website, integrating titles in your catalog, and having to pay setup fees may be nonexistent or at least negotiable. Your vendor may or may not require you to have a stand-alone website for the e-books you buy from it. As part of its service, the vendor may create and host a website for your e-books that you'll link to from your own website. An example is OverDrive (http://www.overdrive.com/), which can create a custom website for libraries that it calls a "virtual branch." Other vendors may merely provide a list of e-books titles that you can post on your website or integrate into your online catalog for patrons to click on to access the book.

Decisions regarding integrating the e-book titles into your library's online catalog will most likely be left to you. To integrate the titles into your online catalog, you'll need to get MARC records for the titles. The vendor may provide the MARC records as part of its service, or you may have to pay an extra price for them. Integrating MARC records for the e-books into your online catalog will allow patrons to see the e-books as they search your catalog, thus providing another access point to the e-books along with the list of titles on your website or the link to the e-book stand-alone website.

Set-up fees are sometimes nonexistent, depending on the vendor. Some vendors will charge you an amount of money to cover various costs of doing business with them, or they may merely charge you for the e-books. And sometimes vendors may charge or not charge set-up fees based on the type of e-book services you purchase from them. Weigh all costs accordingly.

Ongoing Costs

Ongoing costs may include one or more of these:

- Annual or monthly vendor support fees to cover, among other services, maintenance and platform hosting fees

- Fees for new services or upgrades
- MARC record costs
- Buying or leasing new e-materials

When deciding to buy or lease e-books, determine what the benefits of each are. Purchased e-books will theoretically be yours forever and will likely be available for a one-time cost. Leased e-books may be available in bundles or singly. One benefit of leasing an e-book is that you can choose to not renew it and put money toward different titles when the lease period is up. Pricing of purchased versus leased e-books varies and may depend on use models. Are the e-books to be used by one person at a time, by several users simultaneously, or by an unlimited number of users? See Chapters 5 and 6 for more information on e-book costs associated with the selection process and budgeting.

Shared Costs: Join an E-Book Cooperative

E-book purchasing cooperatives can be formed to share the costs and the e-books if the vendor you've chosen will work with cooperatives. Compare e-book vendors' policies on libraries forming purchasing cooperatives. A vendor may not allow individual libraries to join together in this way unless those libraries are already part of a consortium or library network that is doing the purchasing. If a vendor will do business with a group of libraries that are not otherwise affiliated, purchasing e-books may then be possible for libraries with smaller budgets that couldn't afford such a collection on their own. If forming a cooperative, administration of the cooperative can be shared as well. You'll need to institute cooperative-wide policies, including deciding who does the purchasing, how much each library contributes, and how to set hold ratios. Plan to set up a governing board for the cooperative to set start-up policies and to deal with any new issues that arise.

Collection development and purchasing of a shared e-book collection can be centralized or handled by each library. If centralizing, you'll set up one account with your vendor and typically one library will do the ordering, with all the other libraries contributing money to a central fund. If collection development and purchasing will be handled by each library individually, each library will have its own account with the vendor and will order materials for the shared collection. When libraries handle their own purchasing, someone appointed by the governing board should monitor purchases to make sure each library is contributing as agreed.

Sharing publicity and training throughout the cooperative saves money and staff time. You can use a portion of each library's payment share to pay for public relations items that will be available to all the cooperative libraries, or you may volunteer a staff member to design the items for all the libraries to share. The same method can be used to pay for staff and patron training materials and for designating a trainer to train at all the cooperative libraries.

Best Practices

Best practices that apply to using e-books in public libraries are similar to best practices that libraries apply to any library issue, although minor tweaking may be required:

- Get staff buy-in.
- Keep current with e-book technologies.
- Share information with colleagues in nearby and/or similar libraries.
- Review new products from vendors.
- Assess your e-collection's performance.

Get Staff Buy-In

Getting staff buy-in should be a top priority from the beginning as you consider creating an e-book collection. This may include merely sharing information with your staff, asking for staff input in how to run the e-book collection, and providing training on e-book technology when needed. Your staff, especially public services staff, will be able to provide insight about what patrons are requesting and can help your library's administration determine whether or not patrons will be interested in e-books. Your technology staff will need to be consulted about how to work with the technical aspects of the e-books, and any other staff departments that will interact with the e-books should be consulted. Once the decision is made to go forward with offering e-books, keep public services staff informed of what will be available in the e-book collection, how it will be available, and how patrons can use the collection. Public services staff can continue to monitor patron feedback and can tell patrons about the e-books. Other staff members in your library should be informed of changes with the e-books to help determine how they will impact staff responsibilities.

Keep Current with E-Book Technologies

E-book technologies have exploded in recent months, so much so that keeping current is vital. It will be virtually impossible to avoid articles and information about e-books, but it is important to go further and actively search for information pertinent to your e-book needs. Sign up for e-book–specific or technology-specific electronic discussion lists and RSS feeds, read blogs about e-books, sign up for your vendor's social media accounts, read general information to keep informed, and attend e-book conferences and webinars if your budget and time allow. Here are some recommended sites to visit:

- TeleRead, http://www.teleread.com/: This site aggregates news about e-books, libraries, publishing, and related topics.
- *No Shelf Required*, http://www.libraries.wright.edu/noshelf required/: This blog is about e-books, audiobooks, and other

digital content in libraries. It combines blog entries, discussions moderated by Sue Polanka, Head of Reference/Instruction at Wright State University, and articles.

- Good E-Reader, http://www.goodereader.com/: This is a news and blog site about all things e-reader.
- *Publishers Weekly* digital news website, http://www.publishers weekly.com/pw/by-topic/digital/index.html: This website covers a wide range of digital topics, including content, copyright issues, and apps.
- International Digital Publishing Forum, http://www.idpf.org/: This is the website for the trade and standards organization for the digital publishing industry.

You'll be looking for news and information about new technologies, your vendor and other available vendors, what publishers do or do not work with public libraries, what controls publishers keep on e-books, what titles are available, what new e-gadgets are on the market, and other topics.

Share Information with Colleagues in Nearby and/or Similar Libraries

Talk with neighboring and similar-sized libraries to gather information about their experiences with e-books. In talking with other libraries you may not only gain information about the e-books industry but also find libraries that want to join forces and form an e-book purchasing cooperative, which will likely save you money and help you consolidate power when working with e-book vendors.

Review New Products from Vendors

Some merit may come from working closely with your e-book vendors. Ask about new services and upgrades they'll offer, and ask to be a beta site if your library has the resources to work with the new technologies. If you are able to help vendors test product, you may get a chance to influence the design of the product, and your library may receive discounts on the products.

Assess Your E-Collection's Performance

Because e-book technology is still relatively new, it is hard to gauge what the usage of your e-books collection will be. Usage may change rapidly from month to month, especially if a new technology is introduced or if your e-book vendors start working with more publishing houses. Patrons are still learning about the technology and will continue to do so for quite some time. Continually monitor your e-book collection's usage statistics and change direction if need be. Chapter 9 discusses e-book assessment methods in more detail.

Conclusion

Introducing a new service to your library is rarely a seamless endeavor. It may be challenging to add e-book service to your library because of shrinking library budgets and because e-books can go against some library staff and patron philosophies that hold tight to the idea that a book is a book only if it is printed on paper bound between two covers. Stay patient and continue to work to introduce e-books to your library—it may help to assure staff and patrons that print books are not going away, that e-books will be just one more option. E-books will only become more prevalent in libraries and society as a whole. Offering an e-book collection is one more way to provide service and remain relevant to your patrons.

References

Burkey, Mary. 2011. "Voices in My Head: Digital Synchronicity." *Booklist* 107, no. 9/10: 62.

Duncan, Ross. 2010. "EBooks and Beyond: The Challenge for Public Libraries." *Aplis* 23, no. 2: 44–55.

Genco, Barbara A. 2009. "It's Been Geometric! Documenting the Growth and Acceptance of eBooks in America's Urban Public Libraries." *World Library and Information Congress: 75th IFLA General Conference and Council.* Submitted July 24; presented August 27. http://www.ifla.org/files/hq/papers/ifla75/212-genco-en.pdf.

Hirtle, Peter. 2010. "May a Library Lend E-Book Readers?" *blog.librarylaw.com* (blog). June 20. http://blog.librarylaw.com/librarylaw/2010/06/may-a-library-lend-e-book-readers.html.

Oder, Normal. 2009. "Mixed Answers to 'Is It OK for a Library to Lend a Kindle?'" LibraryJournal.com, April 7, 2009. http://www.libraryjournal.com/article/CA6649814.html.

Schiller, Kurt. 2011. "The *New York Times* Taking an Interest in Ebooks." *EContent* 34, no. 1: 10.

Selecting E-Books

Joanne Doucette and Amy Lewontin

Introduction: Collecting E-Books

Why collect e-books? E-books bring some unique features to a library collection that cannot be duplicated in a print copy. If your collection is for an academic library, your motivation may be to provide access to books outside of the physical and time constraints of the library building. Your users will have access to materials 24 hours a day, and the books won't wear out. In colleges and universities that provide substantial amounts of online education, the library can provide books for students who never visit campus. E-books can enrich the experiences of students by offering a variety of online supplemental texts for those who otherwise might read only the required textbook for a course. In addition, uniquely digital materials often have added value. In place of the standard monograph, the library might purchase an e-book that features frequent updating, embedded media (e.g., videos, podcasts) and embedded links to other online sources.

As a public librarian, you may be motivated to acquire e-books because the public is infatuated with technology, such as e-readers, which have sales projected to double between 2012 and 2013 (Maisto, 2010). As owners of e-book readers, library patrons are looking for free access to current titles to supply their devices. E-books can also extend your services to physically challenged patrons. Those unable to visit the library will be able to access books from home. In addition, the ability to enlarge font size in many e-books will make more of your collection available to the elderly and visually impaired patrons without requiring additional purchases of large-print books. Some e-book systems will even convert text to speech and serve as a talking book. Librarians should not miss the opportunity to add this new exciting format to their collections. This chapter covers some of the basics for acquiring and collecting e-books in a variety of libraries. It also discusses some of the ways e-books are accessed and the various devices that are currently available in the marketplace. Knowledge of the variety of purchasing models will be helpful as you shift your collection from print to electronic.

Defining the Collection

What parameters should you consider when building your e-book collection? Will the e-book collection differ significantly from the traditional print collection? In traditional collection development, aspects of subject coverage, scope of the collection in both comprehensiveness and currency, and appropriate level for the reader are important considerations. E-books are more complex in that their purchasing models have an impact on the nature of the collection. To define the e-book collection, these features are discussed in the following sections.

The Nature of E-Books

While traditional collection building is usually the result of the selection of appropriate titles, the nature of building an e-book collection can be quite different. The ability to select a title is often affected by how the publisher or aggregator offers the e-book for purchase. Following the style of e-journal acquisition, it is not always possible to purchase an individual title. Collecting e-books will add a new dimension to your collection—subject or aggregated collections of e-books. E-books are usually sold in three ways: (1) selected individual books, (2) publisher subject collections, and (3) aggregator collections offering titles from multiple publishers. Defining your collection will now include individual collections of e-books in addition to individual titles. Accepting that you must work within this more complicated model, you can now begin to evaluate e-books using the traditional features of subject, audience, scope, and currency that define your collection.

Subject Coverage

Are e-books the correct format for every subject in the library? It will be important for you to evaluate these factors:

- How e-books are used
- Expressed user preference
- Quality of reproduction
- Availability

Academic libraries are still collecting many print books in the fine arts and social sciences due to the desires of faculty, the difficulty in locating e-books with acceptable image quality, and the delay in the publication of materials in e-format. Science, technology, and medical (STM) books were released earlier in the e-book revolution and are generally more available for selection in electronic form. Also, the way that patrons read books can vary by subject or discipline. How someone approaches literature in contrast to a technical report can be radically different. In a subject like medicine, it is rare that a patron will read an entire book. Most users of medical books seek a quick answer in a few paragraphs or chapters. In contrast, studying literature usually requires reading and rereading significant amounts of text. Public library patrons are more likely to want an entire book and prefer a mobile platform (for use out of the library), which provides them with an experience similar to checking out print books for several weeks. If you are a subject specialist for your library selecting topics that are normally approached by reading a chapter (e.g., sciences, technology, reference resources), you are likely to find satisfied patrons by selecting e-books in either web-based or portable platforms. If the entire book must be read (e.g., literature, social sciences, popular fiction), the e-book may be preferred in a portable platform (i.e., smartphones, e-readers) as opposed to content hosted on a website. When an e-book or its platform increases the difficulty in using or accessing a book, it is probably not the correct choice for your library.

The quality of digital reproduction is an important feature to consider when selecting e-books. If your subject is image intensive, such as art history, it will be important to evaluate the quality of images provided in the e-book. Some e-book platforms require scrolling to view an individual page. Images are often reduced to thumbnail links to a full image. The full display may not be sized to fit onto the computer screen or e-book reader. Without the ability to resize the image, its impact will be reduced. Limited resolution of the digital reproduction may also limit the usefulness of images in the fine arts. You may also see quite a difference in print quality between e-books that are scanned reproductions of print copies and e-books that are born digital. Make sure that both the text and images will be acceptable to the intended e-book audience before making the purchase.

Scope and Currency

Should e-books be your sole source within a subject? It may not be possible to provide e-books at every level of a research collection. Publishers may not produce e-books for some highly specialized areas, and not all academic press publishers are able to convert to e-format. To reach comprehensive coverage, a mixture of formats (print and electronic) will probably be required. Public libraries may wish to continue to purchase print in addition to e-books because of demand of their constituents and their potential lack of access to or willingness to use technology. If you are a public librarian, you may also find that not all publishers are providing e-books for libraries. At present, two of the "big six" publishers, Macmillan and Simon & Schuster, are selling e-books directly to the public but are not making them available to libraries (EarlyWord, 2011; Miller, 2011). When a popular title is desired from these publishers, you might be able to purchase only print copies. Given the pressure to compete with other publishers, it is likely that this will change in the near future. Until e-books are available at every level of the collection, it may be necessary to select some titles in print.

How important is it for your library to have the most current edition of a book? Many editions of a book may be available in electronic format for individual purchase or in bundled collections. A focused publisher's collection of e-books (e.g., McGraw-Hill's AccessMedicine) can provide access to the most recent edition of the e-book (unfortunately, these may still lag behind the print editions by several months). You may wish to pursue the most current editions if you provide medical or technical information, which can become outdated rapidly.

Some aggregator collections (e.g., ebrary's Academic Complete) may contain older editions of some texts. A quick examination of the publication dates of books included in such collections may demonstrate a lack of publications from the present year. Ask the vendor if there are limitations on the currency of books in the collection because of publisher availability or license agreements. The advantage to purchasing such a collection is the wealth of e-books on many subjects, and the package may be less expensive. The disadvantage is that users may access an older edition of a book and miss updated information that may be available from an e-book purchased through another vendor or from a print copy.

If you are concerned with currency, a discussion with your e-book vendor should provide an estimate of the lag time between publication of the new print edition and the equivalent e-edition. If you feel that the lack of access to current information will have a significant impact on your users, you will need to purchase both print and electronic editions. Purchasing models including ownership, that is, perpetual access, and subscription are addressed in detail later in the chapter. Appropriate employment of these models will help you to control the currency and the cost of your collection. As always, the cost of maintaining a current collection will impact the breadth of books that can be purchased. As the collection development librarian, you will need to balance currency and cost when selecting individual e-book titles and bundled collections.

If you wish to retain older editions of your e-books in addition to adding the most current edition, you should check with your e-book provider regarding perpetual access to older editions. Some publishers simply update information annually and do not have a model to support access to older information (e.g., the electronic version of the *Physicians' Desk Reference* [PDR] provides e-content through a continuously updated web database, unlike the print version of the PDR that has maintained an annual published edition). In these cases, you may find it necessary to purchase print copies to ensure access to older information. Third-party support is available to access older editions of e-books even when publishers are no longer in business. For a research library that maintains multiple editions of titles, investigation into publishers' offerings and the library's long-term access rights will be essential.

Minimizing Duplication

After deciding to collect e-books, your first question may be, should the book be purchased in both print and electronic formats? When e-book platforms were more difficult to use, libraries often felt that both formats were necessary. What if the e-book was not accessible? Over the past 20 years, this debate has been waged about journal access in academic libraries.

In 2011, most libraries are comfortable providing only electronic access to journals, and this has certainly been shown to be the desired format for patrons. Can the same be said about e-books? As discussed previously, there are good reasons why print books should continue to be part of the collection. Is it ever necessary to buy a book in both formats? Here are a few reasons to do so:

- Print is published before the e-book, and the information is needed at that moment. The e-book is also needed for distant users.

- Exclusive access to the e-book is bundled in a collection (one user per collection). Duplication of access to the entire collection may be too expensive. A supplementary print copy may be needed to increase access to the book (such as needed for course reserves).

- The print book is needed for archival purposes. When e-books are continually updated rather than released in editions, purchasing a copy of the print book for historical information may be necessary. A print copy may also be desirable for larger libraries that may wish to preserve a comprehensive collection for researchers.

- Access to technology may not be available to all. Duplication of books in both print and e-format may be necessary to ensure that all patrons have access; this is especially true for public libraries.

In addition to print duplication, it is easy to duplicate an e-book by its inclusion in several bundles. It is important to evaluate overlap and see if you can reduce copies by swapping books in and out of bundled collections. Ultimately, the budget may dictate what you are able to purchase. If a book is perfectly appropriate in e-book format and the platform is stable and user friendly, it should not be necessary to duplicate the book in print unless the print is needed for archival reasons for a comprehensive or research level collection.

Audience

In addition to ensuring that you select materials of an appropriate level for your audience, the diverse makeup of your readers will provide some direction as to the level of collection that needs to be composed of e-books. If you are an academic librarian, your patrons may wish to use your materials late at night after the library is closed. With the growing development of online education, e-books become an essential way to ensure access to library materials for students on and off campus. Public librarians can also use e-books to serve those who cannot come to the library because of illness or disability. Special e-book features, including text-to-speech and larger font sizes, better serve visually impaired patrons and the elderly than do large-print books. E-books provide better access for all populations.

Collection Development Policy

Your collection development policy should incorporate your decisions about the inclusion of e-books in subject areas and the scope and currency of the e-books in your collection. Keep in mind that because of the bundling of e-book collections your collection may have broader subject coverage and scope than you have traditionally defined. It will also be important to review the policy frequently to include technological changes that may affect your e-book choices. Evaluation of accessibility and deselection criteria will be an essential part of the policy to ensure that both the content and the platform remain relevant.

Selection Process

The e-book selection process can utilize traditional methods of collection development. You will find that some of the techniques used to select print monographs are applicable for e-books. A major difference between print and e-formats is the need to consider concepts like access and usability. The following sections provide you with the tools needed to properly begin the e-book selection process.

Establishing Selectors

Is the job of a selector easier or more difficult in this new e-environment? Selection of e-books can involve the participation of many stakeholders: subject specialists, electronic resource librarians, and library patrons. Subject specialists are still involved in selecting materials based on need, content, author, and publisher, but they must now consider electronic format and usability as well. Electronic resources librarians will examine the licensing and financial aspects, evaluate differences in publisher/ aggregator platforms, and access issues, which are all important considerations in e-book selection. How the responsibility of selection is handled in each library will differ. The role of subject selector may not exist, or a selector may also assume the added responsibility of managing electronic resources. To further complicate the picture, a new model of selection became possible in recent years, patron-driven acquisition. In this model, the patron is offered a choice of possible e-books through the library's online catalog and can influence the purchase of an e-book by his selection. The details of this model are described more fully later in the chapter. With all interested parties working together, the selections made should provide a desired, high-quality, and cost-effective collection of e-books for the library.

Choosing E-Books

The following approaches will assist you in the e-book selection process:

- Examining quality publishers
- Following announcements from publishers and vendors

- Setting up approval plans for e-books
- Requesting trials for an e-book collection
- Consulting patrons through patron-driven acquisition
- Identifying e-book sources for a requested title

Examining Quality Publishers

A good place to begin your search for available e-books will be with publishers with whom you have an established relationship from purchasing print monographs. Many publishers have collections of e-books organized by subject. Some e-books are available for individual purchase or are bundled as subject collections. Publishers may also contribute e-books to aggregators. An e-book aggregator can be any organization that offers e-books through a unique platform. The term "aggregator" is loosely defined but most often refers to organizations offering individual titles or collections of e-books from a variety of publishers rather than the offerings of one publisher. Book distributors (e.g., Baker & Taylor) represent both individual publisher offerings and aggregated collections. Publisher websites contain the most complete information with e-book lists organized into subject categories. Keeping frequent contact with publisher representatives is recommended, as they are often the best source of upcoming publications and the only source for institutional pricing.

Following Announcements from Publishers and Vendors

Next time you attend a library meeting or conference, visit the exhibit area and speak with some publishers and book distributors. Sign up to receive e-mail announcements of new collections of e-books and special deals (e.g., late spring offers to spend your allocated funds by the end of the fiscal year). Good relationships with publisher reps and vendors may open up opportunities that you did not know existed.

Setting Up Approval Plans for E-Books

Much like the traditional approval plans used for print books, some book distributors now provide approval plans for e-books. Some of the current providers of e-book approval plans are Coutts Information Services (Ingram), Yankee Book Publishing/Baker & Taylor, and OverDrive. You can set up an approval plan using the same criteria used for print books—subject, audience, publisher, and price. All e-books selected for approval will be added to the distributor's website where selectors can evaluate and approve, reject, or "wish list" a book. Some distributors set up automatic purchase approvals unless a selector rejects a book, the equivalent of receiving a print book on approval. It is important that any such approvals are reviewed in time to reject unwanted titles. Preferred vendors provide a full-text, time-limited approval period so that selectors can see what they are buying rather than only a description or a few pages of the book. Full-text previews of these books provide greater information than librarians have had available to them in the past. Some approval plans allow libraries to receive notification of new e-books being released that are identified according to the approval plan criteria,

---

APPROVAL PLANS

Pros:
- Awareness of newly published e-books
- Automatic purchase within fixed parameters (optional)
- Full-text preview of e-book

Cons:
- Print may be published first
- Only contracted publishers included
- Publisher may not allow third-party distribution of e-books

similar to slip approval plans for print books. Both types of approval plans are important sources of information about new e-books.

There are some difficulties in the use of e-book approval plans. If your library subscribes to print and e-book approval plans, one difficulty is the possibility of receiving the book in both print and e-book formats. The difference in release time for the e-book might present a problem, because the print book is often released earlier than the e-book. If you prefer to receive an e-book in place of print, known as "e-preferred," arrangements may be made with the distributor to delay sending the print for a limited time period to give the e-book time to become available. Another difficulty of selecting books through an approval plan is being limited to the publishers that are represented by the book distributor offering the plan. Distributors can offer books only from contracted publishers and can sell the publisher's e-books only if authorized by the publisher. Some publishers offer their own e-book platforms (e.g., McGraw-Hill) and do not permit their e-books to be sold through a third party. Direct connection with all desired publishers may still be necessary when they are not represented by your distributor in the e-book market and therefore not included in your e-book approval plan.

Requesting Trials for an E-Book Collection

One useful way for you and your users to take a good look at an e-book collection would be to ask a vendor for a trial. A trial offers the opportunity to evaluate specific e-books for both content and platform features. Some vendors may offer a period of two weeks, but, if possible, try asking for a month or more to give you time for a more thorough review. You and your users will be able to evaluate the material's relevancy, currency, and ease of search. Also, check to see if the material can be read easily and whether it is possible to take notes and to print and download a few pages or the entire book. If you open the trial to your patrons, it is advisable to have them give detailed feedback about the value of the material to them so that it can be incorporated into the selection process. A trial period is a good time to assess the value of the e-book collection and also to decide how much of the material on trial you wish to purchase.

Consulting Patrons through Patron-Driven Acquisition

For years, librarians and library administrators have been measuring their book circulation and have often bemoaned the fact that many books are purchased and yet never circulate. This situation is particularly troublesome in libraries that are faced with increased budgetary constraints. In an attempt to maximize patron usage per purchasing dollar, a new model of selection/purchasing has evolved with the advent of e-books. Known by several names, such as patron-driven acquisition (PDA) or demand-driven acquisition (DDA), this model takes the burden of deciding what patrons want from the subject librarian and transfers the selection of e-books to patrons. Purchase is made after the patron has used the e-book, indicating that the book will be of value to at least some patrons.

With patron-driven acquisition a library can choose to have any number of e-book records placed in the library OPAC (online public

Features Desired by Academic Library Users

- Clear print display (not scanned reproduction)
- Search and browse with speed
- Page fits the display—no scrolling
- Download, e-mail, and print chapters/pages
- Bookshelf features
- Highlight and annotate text
- Supplemental material, such as videos, quizzes, and websites
- Compatible with mobile devices/e-readers

Features Desired by Public Library Users

- Clear print to reduce eyestrain
- Page size maximized to reader display
- Scalable fonts
- Bookshelf features
- Highlight and annotate text
- Social networking capabilities
- Jump from text to value-added features, such as dictionaries, maps, websites
- Compatible with mobile devices/e-readers

access catalog) that are made visible to patrons. When the patron finds a book that may be useful and accesses it through the link in the OPAC, it may be counted as one use of the e-book. If he views the index, or title page, and does not read the book, it would not constitute a use of the book. Printing and downloading a page would, however, be counted as a use. The library sets a "trigger" for a purchase of the e-book. One use of it does not constitute a purchase, but five uses of the book can be the purchase point, depending on the arrangement with the vendor with whom you are working. Currently, several vendors are offering patron-driven acquisition.

Libraries that already have created profiles can now choose part or all of the potential purchases to be designated as patron driven, and records for these e-books are loaded into the OPAC rather than received as books or slips. A few caveats about patron-driven acquisition are worth mentioning. Be careful about setting a budget limit for e-book purchases. E-books are generally more expensive than print books, so it is advisable to set limits on individual book prices that are loaded into the OPAC. Also, the collection may become skewed in the direction of the needs or wants of a few patrons rather than a balance of topics that may more fully represent your patrons as a whole. Finally, as was previously mentioned, not all publishers are working with distributors. Some publishers sell their e-books via only their own platform. If you need to work with certain publishers, see if they offer a patron-driven acquisition purchasing model directly to libraries. On the plus side, there are a number of great advantages to patron-driven acquisition. The available purchase and usage reports on the e-books and the instant access to materials that your patrons desire are two advantages to this model of e-book selection.

Identifying E-Book Sources for a Requested Title

There will come a time when you are trying to find a specific title in e-format. It may be a popular book for a public library or an essential course book for an online class in an academic library. If you know the print publisher, start at its website. You will most likely discover who handles its e-book platform. Be aware that publishers may offer different e-formats for a particular title. Lippincott Williams & Wilkins offers PDF downloadable e-books for individuals while offering web-based editions hosted by the Wolters Kluwer Ovid e-book platform for libraries. Sometimes, the book will be available only through a third-party aggregator platform, for example, EBSCO*host*. It may be possible to purchase one book out of the collection for a platform fee and the price of the e-book. If you are still having difficulty finding a particular e-book, try locating the book in OCLC's WorldCat, the online catalog that contains the holdings of most libraries in the United States. The records found in WorldCat often include books from aggregator collections. WorldCat will give you a starting point. You can contact the aggregator rep and see if the book is available. A combination of website searching and speaking with representatives should determine if an e-book is available and direct you to the appropriate salesperson.

SELECTED PUBLISHERS/ DISTRIBUTORS OFFERING PDA

- Blackwell & YBP (EBL: Ebook Library)
- Coutts (MyiLibrary)
- YBP & Blackwell (ebrary)
- EBSCO (EBSCO*host*)

Selecting and Deselecting with the Help of Usage Statistics

E-book usage data provided to you as a part of your e-book purchase is a valuable asset. You will be able to add and remove titles with a better understanding of the desires of your patrons when you consider the usage statistics. Choosing to keep a rarely used e-book will have a monetary cost, unlike print monographs that just take up shelf space. After selecting a vendor for e-books, ask what type of usage statistics will be available to you and how frequently you can access them. The best way to keep track of how your e-books are being used and accessed is to be able to view your usage data as frequently as you need it. COUNTER (Counting Online Usage of NeTworked Electronic Resources)–compliant statistical data provides a standard for publishers and librarians by providing a clear definition of concepts and terms (e.g., successful request, session, chapter, turnaway). The e-book statistics include reports such as "Number of Successful Title Requests by Month and Title" and "Turnaways by Month and Title" (COUNTER, 2006). Access to COUNTER-compliant data is important to be able to make meaningful comparisons among the different types of platforms that you are offering and how they are being used. You can view the types of data that COUNTER-compliant e-book statistics offer as well as a list of COUNTER-compliant publishers at the Project COUNTER website (COUNTER, 2011). Usage statistics are also an important tool for the ongoing assessment of e-book collections. More information on this can be found in Chapter 9.

The next section provides information on the various purchasing models. Purchasing models can exert a direct influence on what is available for selection. Understanding these models is essential in collecting e-books.

PURCHASING/ACCESS OPTIONS

- Perpetual access to individual titles
- Annual subscription to individual titles or collections
- Collections that allow annual swapping of titles
- Patron-driven acquisition
- Pay-per-view options

Understanding E-Book Purchasing Models

The purchase of e-books and e-book collections offers the collection development librarian and library selectors a bit of a quandary, because e-books are simply more complex to purchase and make accessible than the standard monographs may have been in the past. There are a number of factors to be aware of. One question you may want to ask yourself is whether the e-books you are considering are available as a purchase model where your library will "own" the content or as a subscription model where you will lease access for a year or more. If e-books were a place to live, you would have two options: ownership or renting.

Exploring Perpetual Access and Ownership versus Annual Subscription

Should you "buy" or lease your e-books with an annual subscription? The purchase model chosen for an e-book or collection should support the kind of information you are selecting for your users. If you want to ensure that your users always have the current edition of the book, leasing will provide them with the latest edition as soon as it becomes available. It will be particularly important if new editions are frequently being published and updated during the year. The cost of the lease will be an annual expense. When a book has more lasting value or is published infrequently, buying the e-book may be more advantageous. A major research library may choose to build a comprehensive collection of e-books and consequently benefit from always choosing to purchase the e-book. In libraries whose patrons desire mainly new books or latest editions, a combination of leasing and purchasing may be more advantageous.

Purchasing "perpetual access rights" involves paying for the book once with an additional small annual platform fee to use the book at the publisher's website with customized and updated software. Leasing is ultimately more expensive. You must decide if your budget should be used to support a frequently updated collection or to increase the number of e-book titles available to your users. Depending on the structure of your budget, you may have the money to make an end-of-the-year purchase. E-book vendors often approach libraries at this time of year with deep discounts. Taking advantage of these offers can expand your selections at decreased cost. (Refer to Chapter 6 on licensing and Chapter 7 on budgeting for a fuller discussion.) Ultimately, both models, ownership and subscription, are worth investigating to ensure that you have the opportunity to select all desired titles while you maximize the value of your spending.

Protecting Your Purchases

With so much energy spent on selection and negotiation, it is really important to understand the library's rights should the e-books become unavailable. What does perpetual access to an e-book mean if you have stopped doing business with a vendor or it has gone out of business? Will your books be hosted on a third-party electronic archival website, such as Portico (Portico, 2011), or will you be receiving a stack of CD-ROMs in the mail? Clarify the vendor's contingency plans, and include details of the plans in the license so that you can keep your books on a platform that is accessible to all rather than ending up with a pile of CD-ROMs you cannot use.

If your vendor is an aggregator and handles many different publishers, investigate its rights to the titles in the collection you are purchasing. Will you lose access if the publisher pulls its titles from the aggregator platform? Although it may be necessary to accept annual fees on purchased e-books, try to limit the loss of selected titles by investigating your rights and your third-party vendor's rights with respect to hosted publishers prior to purchase.

Choosing to purchase a title should be contingent on receiving the appropriate answers to the concerns mentioned earlier. As will be discussed in Chapter 6 on licensing, your only guarantee to continued access to purchased titles in a desirable format is to include these clauses in the license that specify what is acceptable to you. If the vendor is unable to agree to your terms, you may wish to cancel the purchase.

Selecting the Appropriate User Access Model

Unlike a print collection, your selections will never be missing from the shelves. Your patrons will assume that the e-book is available to them at all times. Sadly, this may not always be the case. As part of the selection process, you must understand how access is provided to your patrons and select a model that will meet the needs of your community. Vendors offer three possible models of user access. Single user of an e-book or a collection (sometimes known as SUPO, or single-user purchase option) is the most limited form of access. If a book is expected to be popular and desired by many users, you may need to purchase or lease additional access to the title. Investigate the model of multiple simultaneous users (also known as MUPO, or multiple-user purchase option) for those titles expected to receive high use despite the fact that it will likely increase the cost of the product. The third purchase option for e-books and the most desirable is the model of unlimited use. Always ask your vendor/publisher what "use models" are available. The cost differences among the user access models can be significant and can have a real impact on the library's collections budget. For more information on budget considerations, see Chapter 7 on budgeting.

To judge how well your access model is meeting the needs of your patrons, keeping track of e-book usage and in particular the number of "turnaways" that individual e-books are receiving will be important. A turnaway indicates that someone tried to use an e-book but was "turned away" because the user exceeded the publisher's e-book or platform license, which allows for only a fixed number of users to access the e-book or collection simultaneously. If you see frequent turnaways for an e-book over time, you may want to consider purchasing additional copies or asking for more concurrent users. If you are in a negotiating position now, make sure to ask about the ability to add more copies or access as needed.

Exploring the Swapping Model

After selecting a particular e-book collection (e.g., STAT!Ref), you will no doubt find, based on use statistics, that your patrons are very happy with some books and uninterested in others. The ability to swap e-books in a collection gives you a second chance to create a more useful assortment or anthology. Currently, some publishers offer e-book collections in which books may be made available for a given period of time and then "swapped" for a different title. ProQuest is currently working with Safari, a vendor of computer and business e-books. In the Safari model, the library purchases a certain number of book "slots" (Safari, 2011). From Safari's administrative site, access to usage data as well as the "swapping" of e-books can occur. After a six-month period, you can begin to evaluate your e-book usage. There will be some titles that receive heavy use and some that may receive none at all. Rather than leaving books that have been used infrequently or not at all on your platform, you may want to consider removing those books and choosing new titles. The swapping model does require work on the part of your cataloger to keep your OPAC up-to-date and ensure that users do not try to access canceled e-books.

Exploring the Patron-Driven Acquisition Model

As previously described, patron-driven acquisition is a purchasing model in which patrons "select" e-books by choosing them from the OPAC and the library and vendor set the number and kind of uses that trigger a purchase. Selecting a portion of your funding and experimenting with patron-driven acquisition will ensure that you are purchasing some e-books that are being used and collecting some statistics on the desires of your patrons.

Exploring the Pay-Per-View Model

To allow your patrons to have limited access to materials which you do not own, you may be able to set up a pay-per-view model (PPV) with your vendor. These models tend to be customized in what the patron can do with the product, the cost to the library, and the terms of use. Many publishers and aggregators provide a PPV option. Ebook Library (EBL) provides a "short-term loan" in which the patron can download a whole book or just a chapter (Ebook Library, 2011b). Elsevier's SciVerse system offers a PPV service that provides the purchaser 24-hour access to a book chapter (SciVerse, 2011). The patron may then view or download it within that period. The McGraw-Hill collections, such as AccessMedicine, offer PPV individual access to the entire collection for 24 or 48 hours at a reasonable cost (AccessMedicine, 2011). PPV models are worth investigating, because they provide a large collection of e-books for patrons without the cost of purchasing or subscribing to the entire collection. As with patron-driven acquisition, it will be important to limit the amount of funds allocated to support the PPV model.

Now that you understand the options available for purchasing and selecting access to your collection, it is time to think about how your users will read their e-books. E-reader and other display devices, like purchasing models, will have a definite impact on titles that will be available for selection. Knowing the desires of your library community is especially important when considering e-books and their availability on different e-readers.

E-Book File Formats, Platforms, and Display Devices

When you consider purchasing an e-book or e-book collection, you will also need to evaluate how your patrons will actually "read" the content.

Readability and access depend on file formats that encode the contents of the e-books and platforms and display devices, which convert the file formats into text. Public libraries are now offering e-books for popular reading to patrons who have purchased their own e-readers or other display devices or are making the decision to lend content-loaded e-readers (Miller, 2011). Academic users are hoping that e-books can be delivered to them on their multiple mobile devices in addition to the standard web interface via their computers. School librarians and children's librarians may be wondering how to begin offering picture e-books. What was once a choice between hardcover and paperback has exploded into a multifaceted decision that requires an understanding of e-book formats and e-book display options in order to make our selections relevant, accessible, and desired by our patrons.

E-Book Formats

Why is it important to know something about e-book formats? You will find that e-book display devices are not compatible with every format. When you choose an e-book from a vendor, understanding the format will help you choose a book that can be used on your patrons' e-reader devices and ultimately receive more use.

"E-book format" refers to the type of file that stores the content of the e-book. Some files are proprietary and can be used only with a specific device and its operating software; for example, Kindle books cannot be read without the Kindle software. Some files can easily be read by many devices, such as PDF. To control what a user can do with an e-book file, the files are often bundled with software that exerts control over copying files, making changes to files, and even eliminating access to files over time (used in "circulation" of e-books). This type of controlling software, also known as digital rights management software, or DRM, varies with the producer of the e-book and with the manufacturer of the e-reader software or device. Four types of e-book files dominate the field.

Portable Document Format (PDF) is the most familiar file format used in e-books. Some library vendors offer e-books in this format. The file extension is .pdf. PDF files are stored as an image of the page. The problem is that the text in PDF files cannot reflow to fit small screens. As a result, when a PDF file is loaded on a small device, the reader usually has to zoom in for the page to be legible, forcing the reader to scroll left and right to be able to read all of the text on a line. The advantage of PDF e-books is that they are compatible with all computers and most e-readers and mobile devices. They can be bundled with DRM software if desired.

Mobipocket format is written in XHTML and is based on the Open eBook standard. The books can be read on the Mobipocket Reader application. They have an extension of .mobi or .prc. Software that converts other file formats to Kindle-readable files often uses this type of file format.

Amazon Kindle uses a proprietary e-book format based on Mobipocket format. The file extension is .azw. The format allows the file to be locked

---

SOME POPULAR E-BOOK FILE FORMATS

- EPUB
- PDF
- AZW (Kindle)
- MOBI (Mobipocket)

to a user's registered device through DRM software. Kindle apps on the user's other devices can also read this format. Amazon has released a new format, Kindle Format 8, with the new Kindle Fire. This format provides more features for publishers, including improved graphics and formatting capabilities as well as support for HTML5 and CSS3 (Amazon, 2011e). Amazon states that when KF 8 is used on existing e-ink models of the Kindle, all content that was previously purchased using the old MOBI standard AZW files will continue to work.

EPUB format is based on an industry-wide standard of the International Digital Publishing Forum (IDPF). The e-book files have the extension .epub. The EPUB format is probably the most commonly used in downloadable library e-books. It is also compatible with Barnes & Noble's and Sony's e-readers. Adobe Content Server is the software that provides DRM for e-readers and services using EPUB format. EPUB-formatted e-books can be read on any Windows or Mac computer through freely available Adobe Digital Editions software (eBook Architects, 2011).

E-Book Platforms

Most libraries will provide a selection of e-books that are available in either of two platforms: web accessible or downloadable. Many publishers are beginning to provide downloadable versions of what once were just web-accessible contents in response to the increased mobile device market. When you are selecting your e-books, check to see if both platforms are available to maximize access for your patrons.

Web-Accessible E-Books

Academic libraries have been heavily invested in web-accessible e-books for years. They were a natural fit in the academic environment where much communication and instruction took place through college computer networks and courseware products. Academic users were already familiar with e-journals, and information technology departments had developed proxy servers to limit access of licensed products to their community. Public libraries, too, offer web-accessible reference books for their patrons.

In many ways, these e-books are the simplest to work with. A publisher/aggregator platform is chosen. Books available for that platform are selected. Links to the e-books can be placed in the catalog, in a courseware system like Blackboard, or on a webpage. The platform software controls what the user can do with the book, including downloading, printing, e-mailing sections, and in some cases adding notes or highlights. While any device that can surf the web has access to the books, the web-based platforms have been slow to offer access to their products through mobile device apps, but this situation seems to be changing.

Downloadable E-Books

Downloadable e-books dominate the consumer e-book market. Popular books and textbooks are available to individuals in either a purchase model for the former or a yearly lease for the latter. Books in the public domain can be downloaded from many sources for free. Downloadable library books usually work with two different models. Public libraries and some academic libraries offer e-books that can be checked out for a fixed period, and then access is removed through DRM software. Most e-books in academic libraries act more like journals, offering book chapters that can be downloaded and retained permanently by the patron.

Are there currently downloadable e-book services that will work with all the different types of e-book readers and mobile devices that your patrons may have? OverDrive (2011) is one such company that works with libraries. OverDrive e-books are accessible through its apps for computers and mobile devices. The borrowed e-book can be checked out to an e-reading device and will be automatically removed through Overdrive's DRM features at the end of the borrowing period.

Adobe also provides software systems for downloadable e-books. Adobe EPUB e-books and Adobe PDF e-books are read through Adobe Digital Editions software. This system is compatible with many e-readers (Adobe, 2011). Many public libraries offer both OverDrive and Adobe e-books to their patrons. Providers of academic content are quickly developing mobile apps to allow patrons to download portions of their e-books to multiple devices. Currently, EBL (Ebook Library) offers a collection of downloadable academic and research books. In the EBL system, the patron can download the entire book for a fixed period set by the library. Their Non-Linear lending is based on 325 24-hour loan periods per purchased book per year (Ebook Library, 2011b). The loan periods can take place simultaneously so that many people, for example, a class, may be able to use the book for a few weeks. EBL has also designed its system to work with various e-reader devices by offering both PDF and EPUB formats (Ebook Library, 2011a). Both web-accessible and downloadable platforms should be considered in every purchase. Some collections will allow both platforms, providing maximum usability for library patrons.

E-Book Display Devices

With what devices will your e-books work? E-book readers? Mobile devices? Will you need an "app"? When making an e-book selection, look closely at the downloading instructions that your vendor offers, and check the compatibility of devices. EBSCO's EBSCO*host* offers a page that very clearly describes the devices with which its e-books are compatible (EBSCO, 2011). Make additional devices known to a vendor if your users are not finding the ones they need. There are still several vendors not yet making their e-books downloadable. If you don't see the downloadable devices you are looking for, remember to ask the vendor if the titles are compatible/downloadable and, if not, when they will be.

E-Book Readers

An e-book reader (or e-reader) is an electronic mobile device that enables you to read digital books, magazines, and newspapers. Most e-readers now run on the Linux operating system, although a few run on Windows 7 and Windows CE. Newer devices are beginning to include color touch screens as well as Wi-Fi, and readers connect to the Internet wirelessly to download books. Some also have 4G capability (the latest version of cellular mobile telephone technology), allowing you to download books wherever you are. One advantage for users is that most vendors allow e-book readers to be purchased without any annual contract, monthly fee, or obligation to purchase. As many people purchase e-book readers, libraries, especially smaller ones, are struggling to keep up with the demand (Bolkan, 2010). The e-reader market is growing exponentially, and manufacturers are trying to meet the demand by creating new e-readers with more advanced features. Table 5.1 is a snapshot of commonly available e-readers in mid-2011.

Table 5.1. Some Currently Available E-Book Readers

Name	Manufacturer	Display	Connectivity	Keys/ Touch	Screen Size	Battery Life	Features	Cost
Kindle	Amazon	E-ink	Wi-Fi	Keys	6"	1 month	E-mail, USB	$79
Kindle Touch	Amazon	E-ink	Wi-Fi	Touch	6"	2 months	E-mail, USB	$99–$139
Kindle Touch 3G	Amazon	E-ink	Wi-Fi or 3G	Touch	6"	2 months	E-mail, USB	$149–189
Kindle Keyboard	Amazon	E-ink	Wi-Fi	Keys	6"	2 months	USB	$99–$139
Kindle Keyboard 3G	Amazon	E-ink	Wi-Fi or 3G	Keys	6"	2 months	USB	$139–$189
Kindle	DX Amazon	E-ink	3G	Keys	9.7"	1 week	USB	$397
Nook Touch Reader	Barnes & Noble	E-ink	Wi-Fi	Touch	6"	2 months	None	$139
Nook Color	Barnes & Noble	LCD	Wi-Fi	Touch	7"	8 hours	Apps and web browser	$249
Reader Wi-Fi	Sony	E-ink	Wi-Fi	Touch	6"	1 month	Wireless public library access	$179
Reader Daily Edition	Sony	E-ink	3G or Wi-Fi	Touch	7"	10–22 days	Web browser and audio	$299
eReader Touch	Kobo	E-ink	Wi-Fi	Touch	6.5"	1 month	None	$130

Source: Data compiled from Amazon, 2011b; Amazon, 2011c; Barnes & Noble, 2011a; Barnes & Noble, 2011b; Sony, 2011a; Sony, 2011b; Kobo, 2011.

Amazon's Kindle is a popular e-book reader offering six models and the new Kindle Fire that is covered later in the section on tablets (Amazon, 2011c). Kindles are now available in keyboard and touch models with both Wi-Fi and 3G connectivity. Part of Kindle's popularity is due to the selection of over one million books that is available through Amazon's online Kindle store and people's familiarity with Amazon (Amazon, 2011c). You can download an app for PCs and most mobile devices to continue to read your Kindle books on any device. Kindle's recent entry into the library world through a partnership with OverDrive has expanded options for Kindle owners (Amazon, 2011a). Kindle has also just released the Kindle Owner's Lending Library for individuals who subscribe to the Amazon Prime service. This "library" provides a free e-book each month along with other benefits. The cost of the service is $79 per year (Amazon, 2011f).

Barnes & Noble's Nook e-book readers and Nook tablet are also very popular and have a large selection of books available for purchase through Barnes & Noble's online Nook store. Your patrons can borrow books from your library to read on their Nook because of its compatibility with standard e-book formats like EPUB. They can also read their Nook books by downloading the Nook application software for PC and mobile devices (Barnes & Noble, 2011b). The Nook Color is appropriate for picture books, and some special interactive picture books have been developed specifically for it. The color screen also provides more lifelike reproductions of e-magazines and e-newspapers (Barnes & Noble, 2011a). By allowing customers to interact extensively with its e-book readers in their stores, Barnes & Noble has given the reader confidence in the product prior to purchase, an advantage over Amazon's Kindle.

Other widely available e-book readers include those produced by Sony, which are compatible with multiple file formats including MP3 and Kobo e-book readers. Both of these manufactures have created devices that can read many e-book formats and are compatible with library e-books.

What makes e-book readers so popular?

- Customizable displays—adjust font size/style and text layout
- Portability—small and lightweight
- Capacity—thousands of books in one device
- Clarity—e-ink technology prevents eye fatigue and allows reading in any environment
- Long battery life—some devices work for months on one charge

Features of e-book readers that make for a quality reading experience are shown in the sidebar. Also offer your patrons a possible checklist so that they can evaluate the readers.

Smartphones for Reading E-Books

Smartphones such as iPhone, BlackBerry, Android, and Windows phones can be used as devices for reading e-books. Many apps exist to

---

E-BOOK READER CRITERIA

- Ease of use and navigation
- Touch-sensitive screen
- Removal storage options
- Text-to-speech features
- Lighting/readability for both indoor and outdoor and nightlights
- Battery life
- Screen size
- Memory capability

enable readers to view as well as download e-books directly to their phone. As previously stated, both Kindle and Nook provide access to their books through free apps for most smartphones.

One example of an app for e-books offered by libraries is the OverDrive Media Console app available for many smartphones. As previously described, OverDrive is a distributor of downloadable e-books and audiobooks with more than 500,000 digital titles from over 1,000 publishers available to libraries (OverDrive, 2011). Patrons can use the app to locate a library that offers digital books and then download e-books and MP3 audiobooks directly through the app. E-books acquired from the library automatically expire after a fixed time period and contain customization options like resizing text, bookmarking, and changing the brightness of the display. Mobipocket Reader is another free app available for many smartphones, in particular BlackBerry. Mobipocket e-books are available through many libraries, and the reader can customize the display in the usual ways (Mobipocket, 2011).

Tablets

Tablets are the latest mobile devices that can serve as e-book readers. Apple's iPad 2 has an LED back-lit display. While it lacks the flexibility of reading with e-ink, one distinct advantage of the iPad as a book reader is the beautiful color graphical display. The larger 9.7-inch touch screen enhances viewing illustrations in e-books and children's books and improves the experience of reading newspapers and magazines. The battery life of the iPad 2 (10 hours) is much shorter than that of other e-readers, which may make it less popular for long trips when the battery may need frequent recharging. As an e-book reader, the iPad suffers slightly from its back-lit display that makes it difficult to read in brightly lit or outdoor environments. The cost of an iPad ($499 for Wi-Fi, higher for 3G) makes it an expensive e-book reader. The added features of web surfing, apps, and tablet staples such as video and still cameras may offset the cost if one is willing to invest (Apple, 2011). At this point in time, competitors are scrambling to match the iPad's superior display and gain a share of the market (see the comparison table compiled by Franklin, 2011). Samsung has several tablets on the market, including the Samsung Galaxy Tab 10.1, a leading Android-based competitor to the iPad (CNET, 2011a). Sony has recently released the Sony Tablet S, also Android based (CNET, 2011b). The most threatening competition to the iPad may be the recently released Kindle Fire tablet by Amazon (Amazon, 2012d). Priced for initial release at $199, the Kindle Fire is a smaller and lighter device (7-inch display, 14.6 oz) and may be very popular with those interested in purchasing a tablet. Barnes & Noble has similarly released the Nook tablet with comparable size, weight, and features to the Kindle Fire (Barnes & Noble, 2012c). The initial cost is $249. The tablet market is constantly changing. You can find out information about the tablets that are available when you are ready to purchase by following publications like *PC Magazine* or *New York Times* and websites such as CNET.com and other dedicated technology review websites—or even Wikipedia.org, which is frequently updated.

Overwhelmed? The knowledge required to make appropriate e-book selections for your library seems to grow by the day. Keep up-to-date by following some of these suggestions:

- Take advantage of your selection team members and your electronic services librarian to provide good vendor relations and the options available in vendor packages.

- Keep abreast of new developments in e-books through blogs, electronic discussion lists, the media, and conversations with your vendors.

- Read the professional literature and attend conferences.

- Talk to your patrons. They know how they would like to read their books. Ask to look at their mobile devices and get as familiar with new technology as possible. You'll get some free education and some tips on what you should be looking for in the selection process.

- Purchase staff e-readers/tablets to become familiar with these products and how they operate. If your library is unable to afford these devices, visit retail shops to try out the devices.

Budgetary and Licensing Concerns

Selection of e-books should always take into account aspects of budgeting and licensing. While budgeting and licensing will be covered in detail in Chapters 6 and 7 of this book, this section provides a short introduction to assist you in your e-book selections. Budget and licensing considerations are vitally important, because these factors often override other selection criteria.

Cost Considerations That Impact Selection

If the price of the e-book, collection, platform, or concurrent user fees is prohibitive, then the selection may not be economically feasible. The reality is that individual e-books are more expensive than their print counterparts, so you may find that your book budget has less purchasing power in the e-book world. If your collection was well selected, you will find that more of your e-books are getting used than their print counterparts by providing reading mobility and remote access 24 hours a day. As previously stated, watching usage statistics and tweaking the collection each year will help you gain the best use of your dollar. The following are some concepts to think about as you build your e-book collection.

Maintaining an extremely current collection is most efficiently handled by choosing a leasing option to ensure that you always have the most recent edition of a book. You will be effectively spending your budget to support upkeep on a limited number of titles. By contrast, one-time purchases are relatively cost-free to maintain after initial purchase. Most libraries will use a combination of these purchasing models to maximize their funds.

The costs of e-book platforms used in most academic libraries follow several different models. When perpetual access is acquired, the e-book is treated like a print book. For two people to access the book at the same time, two "copies" must be purchased, usually at double the cost. When e-books are leased in a collection of books, the vendor may offer several models of access. The most limited access, and thus the least expensive, is to purchase one "seat" to the collection. Only one person may access the collection at one time. You can purchase multiple seats to the entire collection at greater cost. Other models will charge for access to the entire collection, but, once purchased, you can add additional user access to individual titles. The additional cost is greatly reduced, because you are "buying" an extra copy of one of the books, not the whole collection. Many collections (e.g., ebrary) offer unlimited user access. The price of the collection is then based on the number of potential users. In academic libraries, this number is usually the entire student body and faculty. If the collection is highly specialized, you may be able to negotiate with the vendor to base its price solely on the population of those who will realistically be using the collection, such as a particular program or school (i.e., school of nursing). Discussion and negotiation with vendors is always important. Prices for collections are flexible. If you are unable to afford a desired collection, the vendor may work with you to find a reasonable compromise. Ultimately, you want to select the best collection of titles with the appropriate level of user access to make your collection of e-books beneficial and not frustrating to your patrons.

Licensing Issues That Impact Selection

Licensing is always a big part of acquiring any digital product. The topic is covered in Chapter 6. It is important to review every license received, as changes may be made without notification to you. Remember, negotiation is important and expected. Ask for what you want, and do not accept terms that will make the product too restrictive for your patrons' use. If the publisher is not willing to consider a license that better fits your institution, then selecting e-books from that publisher or vendor may not be in your best interests. To aid in the selection process, the sidebar will give you the basic components to look for in a license.

Conclusion

You now have the tools to begin developing your collection of e-books. Locating books that match your library's profile will involve conversations with your selection team, discussions with vendors, and online research. You will need to examine purchasing models and usage statistics to decide on a cost-effective collection that meets your users' needs. Being aware of issues to discuss before you sign the license may help you to negotiate with more confidence. Armed with an understanding of e-book display options, you can discuss mobile devices or e-book readers with

BASICS OF LICENSING

When?
- What is the period covered by the license?
- When is payment due?

Who can use it?
- Who in your community can use the e-book?
- Can library guests use it under any circumstances?
- Can you lend the e-book or parts of it to others through interlibrary loan?

How can it be used?
- How can the e-book be used in addition to being read by a library patron?
- Can patrons download the book to a computer or mobile device? Print a chapter? Send sections through e-mail? Share with a research colleague?
- Can the e-book be downloaded to a courseware system? Put on e-reserve?
- Can parts of the e-book be used for posters or presentations?

What are the rights of the library?
- Is the library protected from unauthorized uses by patrons if the library has made appropriate efforts to prevent such uses?
- Are there any special areas where liability may be an issue?
- Will the publisher provide archival copies of any books purchased if its platform or business ceases?

your patrons to see which e-book formats will provide content for their devices. As with all technologically based products, expect change and keep informed to make the best selection of e-books for your library.

Selecting traditional print books involves the process of looking at the book subject, the reputation of the author and publisher, the readership level and intended audience, and, finally, the cost. As discussed in this chapter, selecting e-books also includes added factors of licensing (more fully discussed in Chapter 6) and access issues, new publishing models, more complex cost considerations (see Chapter 7 for more detail), and the ever-changing world of e-readers and new handheld devices.

References

AccessMedicine. 2011. "AccessMedicine Subscriptions: Pay Per View." AccessMedicine. Accessed November 8. https://store.accessmedicine.com/homePPV.aspx.

Adobe. 2011. "Digital Editions Supported Devices." Adobe. Accessed September 19. http://blogs.adobe.com/digitalpublishing/supported-devices.

Amazon. 2011a. "Borrow Kindle Books from Your Local Library." Amazon. Accessed November 8. http://www.amazon.com/gp/feature.html?ie=UTF8&docId=1000718231.

———. 2011b. "Kindle DX." Amazon. Accessed September 19. http://www.amazon.com/Kindle-DX-Wireless-Reader-3G-Global/dp/B002GYWHSQ.

———. 2011c. "Kindle E-Readers." Amazon. Accessed November 8. http://www.amazon.com/Kindle-eReader-eBook-Reader-e-Reader-Special-Offers/dp/B0051QVESA/ref=amb_link_358679582_2?pf_rd_m=ATVPDKIKX0DER&pf_rd_s=center-1&pf_rd_r=0TE1PPPKK880HX0R4794&pf_rd_t=101&pf_rd_p=1329990322&pf_rd_i=507846.

———. 2012d. "Kindle Fire." Amazon. Accessed January 23. http://www.amazon.com/dp/B0051VVOB2/ref=sa_menu_kdpo3.

———. 2011e. "Kindle Format 8." Amazon. Accessed November 9. http://www.amazon.com/gp/feature.html?ie=UTF8&docId=1000729511.

———. 2011f. "Kindle Owner's Lending Library." Amazon. Accessed November 8. http://www.amazon.com/gp/feature.html/ref=amb_link_35867 9582_5?ie=UTF8&docId=1000739811&pf_rd_m=ATVPDKIKX0DER&pf_rd_s=center-1&pf_rd_r=0Z1VRKJ2XMHMY3X7FMPC&pf_rd_t=101&pf_rd_p=1329990322&pf_rd_i=507846.

Apple. 2011. "iPad Features." Apple. Accessed September 19. http://www.apple.com/ipad/features/.

Barnes & Noble. 2011a. "Nook Color—The Reader's Tablet." Barnes & Noble. Accessed September 19. http://www.barnesandnoble.com/nookcolor/index.asp.

———. 2011b. "Nook—Features." Barnes & Noble. Accessed September 19. http://www.barnesandnoble.com/nook/features/index.asp.

———. 2012c. "Nook Tablet—Specs." Barnes & Noble. Accessed January 23. http://www.barnesandnoble.com/p/nook-tablet-barnes-noble/1104687969.

Bolkan, J.V. 2010. "Product Reviews: E-Book Readers." *Learning & Leading with Technology* 38, no. 2: 40–43.

CNET. 2011a. "Samsung Galaxy Tab 10.1" CNET. Accessed September 19. http://reviews.cnet.com/tablets/samsung-galaxy-tab-10/4505-3126_7-34505338.html.

——. 2011b. "Sony Tablet S." CNET. Accessed September 19. http://reviews.cnet.com/tablets/sony-tablet-s-16gb/4505-3126_7-34847717.html?tag=mncolBtm;rnav.

COUNTER. 2006. "The COUNTER Code of Practice: Books and Reference Works, Release 1." The COUNTER Project. Accessed October 19, 2011. http://www.projectcounter.org/cop/books/cop_books_ref.pdf.

——. 2011. "COUNTER—Online Uses of Electronic Resources: Registers of Vendors." The COUNTER Project. Accessed September 19. http://www.projectcounter.org/articles.html.

EarlyWord. 2011. "S&S CEO on Ebooks in Libraries; Size of Ebook Market." EarlyWord. Accessed November 8. http://www.earlyword.com/2011/03/24/s-size-of-ebook-market/.

eBook Architects. 2011. "eBook Formats." eBook Architects. Last modified June 6. http://ebookarchitects.com/conversions/formats.php.

Ebook Library. 2011a. "EBL Adds 30,000 EPUB Ebook Files for Enhanced Download." Ebook Corporation. Last modified June 22. http://www.eblib.com/?p=news&i=5110.

——. 2011b. "Introducing Ebook Library: Technology in the Service of Knowledge." Ebook Corporation. Accessed October 19. http://www.eblib.com/pdfs/ebl_brochure.pdf.

EBSCO. 2011. "Downloading & Devices." EBSCO. Accessed October 19. http://www.ebscohost.com/ebooks/user-experience/downloading-and-devices.

Franklin, Eric. 2011. "CNET Looks at Current and Upcoming Tablets." CNET. Last modified March 2. http://news.cnet.com/8301-17938_105-20037960-1/cnet-looks-at-current-and-upcoming-tablets/.

Kobo. 2011. "The New Kobo eReader Touch Edition." Kobo. Accessed September 19. http://kobobooks.com/touch.

Maisto, Michelle. 2010. "Desktops and Notebooks News: E-Reader Sales to Nearly Double between 2012 and 2013: ABI Research." eWeek. Accessed October 20, 2011. http://www.eweek.com/c/a/Desktops-and-Notebooks/EReader-Sales-to-Nearly-Double-Between-2012-and-2013-ABI-Research-571601/.

Miller, Rebecca. 2011. "Dramatic Growth: LJ's Second Annual Ebook Survey." *Library Journal* (October 15). http://www.thedigitalshift.com/2011/10/ebooks/dramatic-growth-ljs-second-annual-ebook-survey/.

Mobipocket. 2011. "Mobipocket Reader 5 for Mobile Devices." Mobipocket. Accessed September 19. http://www.mobipocket.com/en/DownloadSoft/ProductDetailsReader.asp?View=Device.

OverDrive. 2011. "About OverDrive." OverDrive. Accessed September 16. http://www.overdrive.com/About/.

Portico. 2011. "Portico—A Digital Preservation and Archiving Service." Portico. Accessed September 19. http://www.portico.org/digital-preservation/.

Safari. 2011. "Simple Subscription Options: Pick and Choose Titles—Even Swap Your Books to Keep Costs Down." Safari. Accessed November 8. http://www.proquest.com/assets/literature/products/databases/safari.pdf.

SciVerse. 2011. "Pay-Per-View." SciVerse. Accessed November 8. http://www.info.sciverse.com/sciencedirect/buying/individual_article_purchase_options/ppv.

Sony. 2011a. "Reader Daily Edition." Sony. Accessed September 16. http://
store.sony.com/webapp/wcs/stores/servlet/ProductDisplay?productId
=8198552921666258035.

———. 2011b. "Reader Wi-Fi." Sony. Accessed September 16. http://store
.sony.com/webapp/wcs/stores/servlet/ProductDisplay?catalogId=10551
&storeId=10151&langId=-1&productId=8198552921666384231#
overview/.

Licensing of E-Books

Becky Albitz
and David Brennan

Introduction

Electronic resources have been a part of library collections for well over 20 years, and electronic books have been part of that electronic information landscape for just as long. Some of the very early electronic resources, in fact, were books, such as Early English Books Online and Project Gutenberg. With this in mind, it might seem that all conceivable licensing issues would have arisen and been addressed already, including those that perhaps might be considered unique to the digital book. Most have, but with every new product, access method, and publisher model come new variations on some very familiar themes. This chapter addresses the licensing issues that the new iteration of electronic books has created. Some of the issues raised are themselves not new but have different implications when applied to monographic content. E-book licensing is changing so rapidly that capturing all possible iterations would not be possible. This chapter attempts to provide guidance in addressing issues related to licensing of current e-book offerings. It is possible that the publishers used as examples may have changed their models between the time this chapter was written and when it is published. This chapter focuses on licensing models aimed primarily at an academic audience.

Licensing E-Books

Licensing of e-books in many ways is no different than licensing of the other electronic resources libraries have been working with for over 20 years. This chapter is not going to address the licensing commonalities among all electronic resources, however, but raise issues that are unique to e-books and the variety of ways in which a library can provide access to and use of this content. These issues include:

- platform decisions and the implications for use;
- differences in use of e-books and print books of the same title in providing standard library services such as interlibrary loan, course reserves, and course pack creation;
- using e-books in different formats (e.g., online, downloadable on an e-reader, etc.); and
- long-term or archival access and preservation issues.

A key point here and one that is also addressed in Chapter 7, on budgeting, is that e-book "licensing" can encompass either:

- outright purchase of a particular title or package with the intent of the library to "own" the right to access the content in perpetuity (which may or may not entail annual maintenance or access fees) or
- a subscription model in which access to titles or packages is subject to annual renewal and the material is not owned by the library.

Platform Decisions

Conceptually, people are used to going to a single location to discover print books—the library catalog. Once retrieved, one book is used just like another; there are no "functionality" or "platform" issues. Libraries and users would like the same to be true for the electronic book, but that just is not the case; multiple ways exist to acquire and access e-books.

Title-by-Title Access on Third-Party Platforms

When selecting electronic books title-by-title, librarians have three options:

- They can purchase directly from the publisher, with access provided on the publisher's website.
- They can purchase through third-party platform providers or aggregators—EBL (Ebook Library), ebrary, EBSCO eBooks (formerly NetLibrary) and STAT!Ref, for example. These are companies that provide an Internet "home" for publishers who do not want to manage their content on their own websites. This model can be coexistent with the first option—some publishers that have their own platform also license content through third parties. Expect this to be a moving target—it will change as licenses between publishers and third-party providers change. A recent example is McGraw-Hill no longer licensing through STAT!Ref.
- They can purchase electronic versions of books through print book suppliers such as Baker & Taylor's YBP and Rittenhouse, which partner with both publishers and third-party platforms to host the purchased content.

The challenge in licensing e-books on a title-by-title basis is that multiple licenses need to be in place to allow the library to build the broadest possible collection. This is the case because some books are available from only a third-party platform provider or directly through the publisher, each of which would require a separate contract. If working through a print book jobber is preferred, the same contracts will still need to be in place prior to placing orders. For example, for an order for an e-book available on EBL to be placed through YBP, a fully executed contract with EBL will have to be on file with YBP.

Because multiple licenses need to be in place for maximum collection options, multiple licenses will need to be negotiated. Negotiating a license with any of the third-party e-book platforms is particularly problematic, as they have a limited ability to alter their terms and conditions to meet your needs. The agreements EBL, ebrary, EBSCO eBooks, or any other content aggregator reach with individual publishers dictate the terms they are able to offer you as the licensee. This means that aggregators have to find commonalities among the varying terms and conditions hundreds of different publishers want in place to govern the use of their digital content. For example, one of these publishers might be willing to permit multiple simultaneous users and the interlibrary loan of a whole book, while another publisher may permit only one user at a time and no interlibrary loan at all. One of the results of this conflict in levels of permissions among publishers is the varying access levels found on third-party platforms:

- Single user at a time access for the equivalent cost of the hardcover book (e.g., EBSCO eBooks, ebrary)

- Nonlinear lending, which allows multiple simultaneous users, but only 325 uses a year, for 100 percent of the cost of the hardcover edition (e.g., EBL)

- Unlimited users for 150 percent of the hardcover cost (e.g., ebrary, EBL)

The best solution for the platform providers is to create licenses that are based on the most restrictive usage rights, knowing that they will be able to satisfy the largest number of publishers. Unfortunately, in order to accommodate those publishers who insist on more restrictive access and usage rights, these contracts contain terms and conditions that are more restrictive than librarians and some participating publishers would prefer. Although there are still sections of the license that can be negotiated, such as what law governs the terms of the contract (jurisdiction) and who is responsible for specified violations of terms in the contract (indemnity clauses), limited opportunity exists to negotiate usage rights such as interlibrary loan and electronic reserves. As the model of licensing individual e-book titles through third-party platform providers matures, however, expect to see licensing terms grow more consistent and, hopefully, more liberal, as they have with electronic journals. This trend can be found in the development of standardized licensing language and in the introduction of the Shared Electronic Resources Understanding (SERU)—an agreement between parties that outlines very general use terms based on U.S. copyright law (http://www.niso.org/workrooms/seru).

Licensing Directly with a Publisher

More flexibility in licensing e-books is available when working directly with the publisher. Publishers are hampered only by the agreements they have with their individual authors and the technical limitations built into their platforms. Therefore, there is more ability to shape an agreement to meet the institution's needs, including, for example, more expansive interlibrary loan, electronic reserves, and scholarly sharing rights. One of the more dramatic licensing differences between publishers and third parties is the user access model. The single concurrent user model is almost universally disliked among librarians and users, but it is the model under which most books are made available on third-party platforms, as noted earlier. The nonlinear lending option through EBL is this company's attempt to find a compromise between some publishers' desire to protect their market share and control the digital version of their work, and address librarian and users' dissatisfaction with the single concurrent user model. On the other hand, the access model in place when working directly through a publisher tends to be the same that has been in place for almost all electronic journals and most databases—unlimited simultaneous users. Of course there are still publishers that maintain the limited simultaneous user model, including McGraw-Hill and Lippincott Williams & Wilkins, but they are rare.

Although there is more flexibility negotiating usage rights and user access terms, buying directly from the publisher can limit the ability to select individual e-book titles. Publishers such as Springer and McGraw-Hill do not provide title-by-title access on their own platforms. E-books must be licensed in subject packages to take advantage of unlimited users, more liberal licensing terms, and flexible pricing options. You are in a stronger position to negotiate pricing when you license a package than you are an individual title. In licensing a subject e-book package, you could conceivably receive more content for less than you would have paid had you purchased individual e-books from the same package. Therefore, you need to decide which model serves your institution most effectively—title-by-title via a third-party platform with more restrictive licensing terms, subject packages licensed directly from the publisher with more licensing and use options, or a combination of these two.

Subscription Packages

Another general model for e-books is the package subscription model. If this option is selected, the library will have access to a database of book content selected by the provider. These e-book collections can be based on a specific subject, such as McGraw-Hill's engineering package, or they can bridge a number of broad disciplinary areas, such as ebrary's Academic Complete. Licensing issues for this type of package will be different from those for purchased e-book content, because the licensee

E-BOOK SUBSCRIPTION PACKAGE MODELS				
	EBL	ebrary	EBSCO eBooks	Publisher
Number of concurrent users	Unlimited	Single user	Single user/three users	Unlimited
Uses a year	325 24-hour uses	Unlimited	Unlimited	Unlimited
Book selection	Title-by-title	Title-by-title or packages	Title-by-title	Subject packages
Cost of book	100 percent of hardback	100 percent of hardback	100 percent of hardback	Discount per title
Access options	24-hour offline download or must be online	Single chapter download or must be online	Must be online	Publisher-specific
Is model negotiable?	No	No	No	Yes

does not acquire any ownership of titles and the content of these packages is not necessarily stable.

The sidebar above gives a snapshot of current e-book package subscription models available from the three primary third-party platforms and those available directly from the publisher. Of course, variations on these models exist.

Licensing and Permitted Uses

Under U.S. law, what you can do with a licensed e-book may be quite different than what you can do with a print book. The First Sale Doctrine allows the physical lending of a book between individuals or, in the case of libraries, via interlibrary loan. Section 108 of the copyright law permits the photocopying and sending of a chapter of a book or a journal article to requesting libraries (http://www.copyright.gov/title17/92chap1.html#108). Putting a physical book on reserve is not an issue at all, based upon copyright or any other law, as it is not copied, but just moved from one location within a library to another. All of these activities, however, become much more complex when utilizing the electronic version of a title. When reviewing a license it is important that the uses you need to make of the electronic version are *permitted*, either explicitly through a statement in the contract that spells out how the content may be used or implicitly by preserving your ability to exercise your rights under copyright law. The issues dealing with downloading content to individual devices or library-owned e-readers are more common in a public library setting and are discussed in Chapter 4.

Interlibrary Lending

Interlibrary lending of electronic books in their entirety is almost unheard of, just as would be the lending of an entire electronic journal issue. The obvious reason libraries are not permitted to lend or borrow whole electronic books is because publishers are concerned that their content will be pirated. Another, less obvious reason for this restriction is that the chapter has become the primary unit in the electronic book, just as the article has always been the unit of interest in the journal issue. The book has become disaggregated, particularly in the sciences and the social sciences where chapters are more likely to stand on their own. The licensing language for e-books reflects this transition. For example, the following contract language from Cambridge University Press is fairly standard when discussing what and how much of an electronic book may be loaned:

> Supply to the library of an institution within the same country as You (whether by post, fax or secure transmission, using Ariel or its equivalent, whereby the electronic file is deleted immediately after printing), for the purposes of individual research or private study by an Authorized User of the library and not for Commercial Use, a single paper copy of an individual document forming part of the Work, provided that the limits detailed in clause 3(b)(ii) and (iii) below continue to apply.
> (b) Authorised Users may, subject to clause 4 below:
> 4. (ii) copy and paste one chapter of each title in the collection in question, or up to 5% of the pages from the total collection, whichever is the greater, for personal use only, during any given four-week period, unless otherwise stated in a collection;
>   (iii) make printed copies of one chapter or up to 20% of the pages from the total collection, whichever is greater, for personal use, during any given four-week period, unless otherwise stated in a collection (Cambridge University Press standard e-book license, unpublished).

Note that in this particular contract the lending library is required to print out the segment to be lent, clearly identified as a chapter, and then mail, fax, or Ariel it to the borrowing library (Ariel is a document transmission mechanism that deletes the digital file once the transmitted content has been printed at the receiving location). A number of journal publishers still require this cumbersome process in order to ensure some degradation of the image and the deletion of the original after transmission, although slowly licensees are being permitted to send a secure digital file, which saves staff time and paper. Other contracts treat e-book chapters as they do journal articles, invoking the CONTU (Commission on New Technological Uses) guidelines to provide parameters for the number of chapters that can be borrowed prior to purchasing the book (National Commission on New Technological Uses of Copyrighted Works, 1979). This is an interesting approach, equating the book chapter with the journal article for the purposes of determining when a library should purchase the book. Librarians will likely resist this model, however, as it increases the record-keeping requirements of borrowing libraries as well as staff workload. A borrowing library may find it more cost-effective to purchase the book after the first interlibrary loan request rather than processing five chapter requests and then purchasing the title. Despite the difficulties in lending/borrowing e-books through interlibrary loan, when negotiating an e-book license, the key is to make sure you retain some right to interlibrary loan the content. Ideally, the license will grant you your rights under copyright law without qualification, allowing you to determine how and how much of an e-book you will lend, but that rarely happens. The license will most likely not permit you to lend the entire e-book and will be proscriptive about how that content can be delivered, but you want to make sure you retain some way to exercise your interlibrary lending rights.

Course Reserves and Course Packs

Permission to utilize licensed electronic content for course reserves and course pack creation is a standard clause in electronic journal licenses and for e-books when the license is directly with the publisher. You are permitted to post a link to almost all licensed content with no concerns whatsoever, and there is general consensus that posting an article on a password-protected website (Moodle, Blackboard, or a library's e-reserve module) for a single semester is also considered permissible under copyright law, as long as the license for the content does not explicitly prevent it. Again, using the language from the Cambridge e-book license, the following permitted uses are frequently found in licenses from publishers:

> (iv) incorporate parts of the Work in Course Packs and/or VLEs (virtual learning environment) to be used by Authorised Users in the course of instruction (but not for Commercial Use) at Your institution and hosted on a Secure Network. Each such item shall be subject to the limits detailed in clauses 3(b)(ii) and (iii) below [see previous quote], and shall carry appropriate acknowledgement of the source, listing title and author of the extract, title and author of the work, copyright notice, and the publisher. Copies of such items shall be deleted by You when they are no longer used for such purpose. Course packs in non-electronic non-print perceptible form, such as audio or Braille, may also be offered to Authorised Users who, in Your reasonable opinion, are visually impaired.

Using content housed on one of the third-party e-book platforms for reserves, however, offers some additional challenges. The single user access model limits the number of students who can utilize the title at a time, which could cause frustration for a large class. Titles that are part of a subscription collection could be removed from the collection mid-semester—a publisher or aggregator's update schedule does not necessarily correspond to the academic calendar! To accommodate such situations, if available, purchase the title rather than lease, and select the multiple user/unlimited uses option.

Institutional licenses govern not just institutional use, but also an individual's use of e-books. After reviewing several e-books licenses, it appears that publishers and third-party providers commonly invoke U.S. copyright law, including the Fair Use doctrine (http://www.copyright .gov/title17/92chap1.html#107). The implication is that an e-book

---

TAKEAWAYS

- Retain ability to use e-books as you can a print book under copyright if possible.
- If not, try to negotiate interlibrary loan rights:
  - Deliver as much of the book as possible.
  - Deliver in digital format if you can to save staff time and resources.
  - Eliminate reporting responsibilities as exist under CONTU.

can be used in the same way as a print version, including permitting limited copying, sharing, and classroom distribution among other uses. However, while the law is not proscriptive about the percentage of a work one can copy and share, the digital rights management (DRM) software e-book providers have included in their platforms effectively limit these amounts. For example, Fair Use could be interpreted to permit an individual to print out two chapters of a book, but the DRM could limit printing to a single chapter. Unfortunately, your ability to negotiate these terms is highly limited or nonexistent, as a content provider would be unable to change the functionality of its site to comply with individual institutional terms. Therefore, prior to agreeing to the license, become familiar with the limitations any provider's DRM imposes on your users, and determine if these restrictions will allow you to utilize the work in a useful manner.

Preservation and Ongoing Access

Finally, if the licensing institution determines that it needs perpetual access to e-book content, the licenses should address the issue of perpetual access and/or preservation. It took a number of years for librarians to feel comfortable about the stability of electronic journals, assisted greatly by the advent of LOCKSS (Lots of Copies Keep Stuff Safe, http://www.lockss.org/), CLOCKSS (Controlled LOCKSS, http://www.clockss.org/), and PORTICO (http://www.portico.org/digital-preservation/)—third-party preservation platforms that ensure that digital content will be available even if the original publisher or provider goes out of business. Preservation (and preservation of access) issues of course vary from library to library and indeed from one subject discipline to another. Where currency is a major issue, such as with medical subjects, preservation of access to a particular edition of a title may be of lesser importance. Indeed, you might desire a licensing model that favors automatic updating of material within a title, effectively making the latest "edition" always the default in terms of access. Escrow arrangements with regard to a publisher going out of business are a concern, more so with serial titles that seem to change publishers on a regular basis.

Preservation clauses are included in e-book licenses, but the mechanism for preservation and ongoing access differs among content suppliers. For purchased content, e-book providers appear to favor two options: providing a stripped-down digital file of book content and/or printing and binding the entire book, the latter being an option that is rarely or ever available for e-journals. Providing a digital file is an option for e-book content purchased from Oxford University Press, Cambridge University Press, and EBL. Oxford in fact offers the option to locally host its content at the time of purchase. Ebrary's license is the only one of these four to explicitly invoke the participation of a third-party preservation partner, although none is named, probably because at this writing the three third-party preservation resources have been slow to include book content in their portfolios. The other option, which EBL and Springer offer, is to print out and bind the book in its entirety. The right of the library to circulate this copy might be restricted—permitted only if the electronic version is no longer available. This option is less desirable for three reasons:

1. Many libraries choose to purchase an electronic version of a book because they have limited physical space in which to house collections.

2. The local cost to print and bind these books could become prohibitive.

3. The workload in determining if access is available and printing and/or retrieving the "archive" copy that would presumably not be in the circulating stacks would be avoided.

Another preservation issue occurs when an e-book is automatically updated online, eliminating the existence of the electronic version of previous editions. In contrast to the example earlier when currency was paramount over retention, those institutions interested in retaining older editions will find that this practice is a challenge for which there is no good remedy except purchasing the print version along with the electronic. Unfortunately this option eliminates some of the benefits of buying the electronic version in the first place, such as space savings and immediate access. In time, more sophisticated methods for guaranteeing perpetual access to this content will likely be developed, probably incorporating it into the existing third-party preservation options, but, as e-books are still evolving, no standard option is currently available.

Conclusion

E-book licensing models are a challenge, one that requires great attention to detail and to the needs of the library and its users in both the short and long term. In contrast to the print environment, where fair use provisions are clearly defined, fair use (and indeed just "use") of e-books can be proscribed by both contractual and technical means. In the academic environment, the following can serve as a reminder of areas to pay particular attention to:

1. Before you begin reading the license, know how the e-book content will be used. This knowledge will inform:
   a. Which platform makes the most sense?
   b. Which use model is most appropriate?

2. Read the license and note:
   a. Is interlibrary loan permitted?
   b. May the content be used for course reserves?
   c. Is there any preservation/perpetual access option available if you are purchasing the e-books rather than subscribing?
   d. If these options are not available, attempt to add them to the contract. You may or may not be as successful as you would like, depending on with whom you are negotiating.

TAKEAWAYS

- If you are purchasing e-books, make sure that a perpetual access clause is in the license and that the preservation mechanism is acceptable.
- If you must retain various versions of a title that is automatically updated in its electronic iteration, consider purchasing a print version for archival purposes.

References

National Commission on New Technological Uses of Copyrighted Works. 1979. *Final Report, July 31, 1978.* Washington, DC: Library of Congress. http://digital-law-online.info/CONTU/PDF/index.html.

Budgeting for E-Books

Becky Albitz
and David Brennan

Introduction

This chapter discusses cost implications for current e-book acquisition options as well as issues arising from access restrictions and changes in collection development and collection funding models. As was seen in the previous chapter on licensing, how e-books are acquired has a direct impact on cost, and that, in turn, impacts the development of funding allocation models to account for these varying modes of acquisition. A traditional fixed allocation for monograph purchases is simply not adequate to the task.

Factors that influence how one budgets for e-books include:

- the access or concurrent user model selected, which could result in either one-time costs or ongoing fees as found in subscription products;
- the decision to lease book content electronically rather than purchasing it outright in print;
- purchasing e-books title-by-title or as part of a collection;
- the simultaneous availability of print and electronic versions of a book, or lack thereof, which increases the possibility of electronic/print duplication; and
- the implementation of library user selection of e-book content, which reduces library control over the e-book budget.

Another budgetary consideration, beyond e-book acquisition, is the issue of libraries purchasing e-readers and tablets. This issue is discussed in Chapter 4 on public libraries and Chapter 5 on selection.

Purchasing Models

A useful way to consider how e-book budgeting is different from other content is to compare it to the evolution of the electronic journal. At their inception, electronic versions of journals were usually "free" with a print subscription—providing electronic access cost libraries no additional funds while allowing librarians and their users to become familiar (and then enamored) with this format. As the e-journal became more popular than its print counterpart, pricing options adapted accordingly. Costs for this content were often "flipped," with the e-journal becoming the primary item purchased and the print version becoming the add-on available at a "deep discounted" price. Finally, as librarians have become more comfortable with the stability and longevity of the electronic versions of journals, the print has, in many cases, been eliminated altogether.

E-books have not demonstrated the same type of relatively slow evolution as electronic journals. Options are not being provided for dual print/online access or deep-discounted print, although there are a few hybrid models in some disciplines—primarily science textbooks. Some print texts still come with an e-book version on CD-ROM, or access is provided to the e-book version and additional content on a "companion website" for which an ID/password can be found in the print book. These hybrids (which are clearly aimed toward the student or individual purchaser and not libraries) are becoming increasingly rare in the general academic arena, although they still appear with frequency in medical titles. In general, librarians are being asked to make a choice—print or online—with few options to help ease the transition beyond expending more money to purchase the same content, only in two different formats. This transition is fraught with a number of budgetary obstacles that will cost more money initially as librarians determine how they are going to operate in the e-book landscape.

Thus, budgeting for e-books is more complicated than budgeting for their print counterparts. Purchasing models for e-books could require an ongoing financial commitment as do serials and databases, a one-time payment like print monographs, or some combination of the two. How you acquire e-book titles or consider publisher business models will have an impact on your budget planning. The distinction here is between these two models:

1. Ownership—purchasing outright on a title-by-title basis, in subject collections, or imprint-year packages using monograph funds (but note that purchased e-books may still have continuing costs attached as an annual payment of some type, generally in the form of a required platform maintenance fee)

2. Leasing through subscription packages or title-by-title from a publisher or aggregator, which requires continuing funds

E-Book Business Models

The business models that are considered in this section are these:

- Firm ordering of individual titles (either leased or owned)
- Subscribing to e-book content in packages (leasing)
- Purchasing e-book content in subject packages (ownership)

Factors to consider when selecting various business models include the following:

- What funds are available (one-time or ongoing)?
- What will the content be used for (research, reserves, leisure reading)?
- Will the content need to be accessed in perpetuity (leased versus owned)?

Title-by-Title Acquisition

In the print world, there are a limited number of ways a library can acquire a physical book. It can be firm ordered, meaning that a librarian intentionally picks the book to purchase. The book can come in on an approval plan, meaning that it meets a set of criteria established in a profile, usually with a prenegotiated discount that results in a measure of savings over the published standard cost. A book title may also be part of a monographic series for which a library has a standing order, and so it arrives automatically upon publication. Only the first option offers complete budgetary control—the cost of the title is known prior to the purchase. The budget impact of the other two options—the approval plan and a standing order—can be predicted but not known exactly, because the number of titles and the exact cost of each cannot be known prior to their receipt. In the print environment all of these options result in the library physically owning the book.

The same models exist for acquiring e-books on a title-by-title basis but with slightly different budgetary ramifications, because the acquiring library may actually purchase the e-book, resulting in the use of monographic funds, or could lease access, which would require ongoing funds if access is to be maintained. As discussed in Chapter 5 on selecting e-books and Chapter 6 on licensing, there are many models for the acquisition of e-books, and these models impact budgeting in different ways. For e-books that are purchased title-by-title, the traditional firm ordering approach—either directly with the publisher, through a third-party platform, or through a book jobber—provides the most control over expenditures. E-preferred approval and standing order plans do not provide as much budget planning stability, but the costs are relatively predictable. Leasing an individual book offers similar budgetary stability in that costs can be predicted, but those costs are annual costs rather than one-time and are subject to inflation, thus costing the library more over the life of the license agreement. This additional cost, however, may be money well spent if the electronic version is used more than its print counterpart would have been. It should be noted that pricing of electronic titles when purchased outright through a book jobber such as YBP does not include the discount in place for print orders, nor does it offer additional savings because there is no paperback equivalent in the digital book world.

Subscription Ordering via Aggregators

Licensed aggregated e-book content, such as is found in ebrary's Academic Complete, a subscription rather than a monographic payment (and subject to annual inflation), offers similar budgeting stability as publisher collections (discussed later). What the subscription aggregation products do not offer is content stability. Because the content is leased, not purchased, the library has no guarantee that specific titles will remain available. When newer editions become available or aggregators end agreements with publishers, content will disappear. Depending on the needs of the library, this may not be a concern. But, if content stability is required, then a copy should be purchased outright, which means that the library will pay more for the same information because it will be in two different formats. Another, more flexible subscription aggregated model is used by ProQuest in their Safari product, consisting of computer manuals, which allows the subscriber to control not only costs but content as well. Titles are assigned a certain number of points, and the subscribing institution decides how many points it would like to license. The subscribing institution then decides which titles it would like to include. The titles themselves can be swapped in and out as new editions are published, but the amount of points paid for remain the same. To further control costs, the subscriber can set the number of concurrent users. As inflation increases the costs of points or seats, the institution can reduce them as needed while still retaining access to the most current technical computer programming content. Currently, Safari is the only product to offer this type of model, but for publishers that offer content with short shelf-lives, adoption of this model would be welcome.

Subject Collection Ordering via Packages

Many publishers offer attractive pricing to encourage libraries to purchase subject packages rather than purchasing individual titles. The publishers see reduced costs in managing access, licensing, and payments, while the libraries can conceivably offer more content to their users for less than they would have paid for individual print or electronic titles. While it is possible to purchase single titles within packages, usually through third-party platforms (which offer no discounting), the cost savings associated with purchasing an entire package can be significant, given some publishers' discount structures. This may not be true, however, in all cases. Some publishers, such as McGraw-Hill, do not permit their content to be sold title-by-title by third parties, and others do not offer substantial savings on package pricing relative to title-by-title costs. No matter what the model, the institutional decision should be driven by a combination of the overall potential intellectual value of the collection, as well as the relative monetary benefits.

The chart in the sidebar (p. 89) provides a general overview of the models available. Compare these models to what was available just within the past decade (Wicht, 2005). There are exceptions to these categories, and options will change as e-book models evolve.

Cost of Concurrent Users

How each title is used will have an impact on acquisition decisions and budgeting. For example:

E-BOOK BUSINESS MODELS			
	Title-by-Title	**Aggregator Package**	**Publisher Package**
Funding	One time for content May have ongoing platform fee	Ongoing subscription	One-time fee[1]
Own or lease	Own	Lease	Own[2]
Cost	100 or 150 percent of hardcover plus annual fee[3]	Annual fee subject to inflation	Discount cost per title—must purchase all titles
Example	EBL, ebrary EBSCO eBooks LWW	ebrary's Academic Complete Safari	McGraw-Hill Springer

1. Except for some publishers, such as McGraw-Hill, that require a subscription for current content.
2. Except for some publishers, such as McGraw-Hill, that lease current content but sell outright archival content.
3. Some publishers allow title-by-title purchasing with volume discounts applied.

- How will the title be used?
  - For reserves?
  - Will people read the entire work or just refer to it briefly?
- Would you have purchased multiple print copies?
- How likely is it that this title will be used by multiple users simultaneously?

As electronic serials publishers have evolved varying concurrent user models, so have e-book publishers and aggregators. NetLibrary (now EBSCO eBooks) first introduced e-book packages in the early 2000s. One of the primary complaints librarians and users had with the NetLibrary platform was that access to a particular title was restricted to only a single user at a time. The concurrent user issue has appeared again with the recent introduction of other third-party e-book platforms. As discussed in the context of licensing and selection, both EBSCO eBooks and ebrary still offer a single concurrent user option, with the cost of those titles the same as the hardcover print version of the work. EBL offers a slightly different approach to this model. While multiple users can access a book at the same time, only 325 uses per year are allocated to each title in their nonlinear lending model for the cost of the hardcover print book. If the freedom and flexibility to offer unlimited concurrent users access to a title with no limit to the number of uses per year is desired, the librarian is required to pay 150 percent of the print cost if the multiple simultaneous user option is an option. The result is less discretion to purchase content overall, because more money is expended on an e-book than would have been spent on its print counterpart. Of course, the opposite could be true if multiple copies of a title would have been purchased in print for reserve use. When content is licensed and delivered on a publisher's platform, pricing tends to be equivalent to the print cost, although this may not be true in specific disciplines such as medicine.

Therefore, in order to provide the most flexibility while still being conscious of financial expenditures, it is important to:

- periodically review usage information,
- consider the number of turnaways your users are experiencing (times when your users are not able to access the e-book because it exceeded the number of simultaneous users as stipulated in the license agreement), and
- adjust your access agreement with the platform provider to accommodate your demonstrated needs.

Print/Electronic Duplication

Clearly, the concurrency question and print/electronic duplication are closely related—if a title is in demand by many users, the librarian will have to decide on the number of concurrent users and if print duplication is warranted. Collection managers wanting to respond to user needs will sometimes be faced with making selection decisions that have real budgetary implications. Factors to consider in regard to print/electronic duplication include the following:

- **Release timing:** Online versions of books still are released after the print version—do you need the title right away, or can you wait?
- **Availability on mobile devices:** Because of digital rights management, most e-books cannot be downloaded to a reader permanently or at all. If users want to read an entire e-book, they will need access to the Internet wherever they intend to read it, which may make duplication in print desirable.
- **Exclusions:** Publishers may not have the rights to offer all of their titles electronically. If you license a subject package, check to see what titles are excluded.

Duplication of book content in both print and online, either intentionally or unintentionally, may occur for a variety of reasons. One reason is due to the different publishing schedules for print and online versions of the same title. A librarian may intend to purchase only an electronic copy of a book, but if the publication of the e-version is delayed excessively, she may choose to purchase the print in response to a specific request and then acquire the e-book when it becomes available. The same scenario may result in unintentional duplication if the publisher does not advertise that an electronic version will be offered.

Publishers that offer their content bundled in subject packages do so because it is more economical for them to manage collections rather than title-by-title sales and access. But inevitably, they are unable to clear electronic rights for some of their content because either the rights cannot be cleared for third-party copyrighted content (such as photos, charts, or graphs) or their authors will not grant electronic distribution rights. This along with differing production schedules can create uncertainty for librarians, particularly if the content in a package is highly valuable or time-sensitive. Because of this uncertainty, librarians may choose to purchase print copies of titles they deem to be critical to their collection rather than discovering at a later date that the same title was excluded from the e-book package. Expenditures on unintentional duplication impact the budgeting process, because there is no way to plan for it. Whatever the reason, any duplication of content reduces the purchasing power of the library and thus is not generally desirable during times of fiscal exigency.

Budgeting for Patron-Driven Acquisitions (PDA)

In contrast to traditional acquisition methods, PDA models remove some budgetary flexibility from the library. For example:

- A deposit account must be established.
- Most funds are expended on rentals, not purchases.
- Each book purchased will cost more than a librarian-selected e-book version or a print version of the same title.
- If a PDA program proves successful, is funding available to replenish the deposit account? Where will this funding come from?

The latest trend in e-book selection, and one with dramatic budgeting implications, is having library users select electronic book titles through their actual use of the content (Sharp and Thompson, 2010). In implementing this model, called either PDA or demand-driven acquisition (DDA), libraries establish a profile for books they would like to make available electronically to their users and create a deposit account with the selected company from which payments for purchased books will be drawn. When a user finds the record for a title of interest, clicks on the link, and remains in the book for a set number of minutes, a use is registered. After a prescribed number of uses, as determined through the negotiation and licensing process, the library officially acquires the title and is billed for it. Each rental prior to the purchase of a title is billed at either 10 or 15 percent of the hardcover purchase price. When purchased, the pricing model for these titles follows the existing policies the selected platform has in place—100 percent for nonlinear use or single concurrent user and 150 percent for multiple simultaneous users. As an example, if it takes three uses to trigger the purchase of a multiple simultaneous user title on ebrary, the library could have paid 180 percent for the book.

Despite the seemingly uncontrolled nature of this e-book purchasing model, there are ways to control costs if so desired. One way some institutions are controlling costs is through the amount they commit to the deposit account. For example, a library may choose to allocate a predetermined amount to an account, and once that money is gone the program is shut down. For those libraries just beginning to experiment with PDA, this is the best way to control costs. Price limits for

CONTROLLING PATRON-DRIVEN ACCESS PROGRAM COSTS

- Limit the amount of the deposit account.
- Place a cap on the price of books included in the program.
- Have a staff member review triggered orders over a certain dollar amount.
- Reduce or increase the number of rentals required for a purchase:
  - The former would reduce costs spent on rentals.
  - The latter would require a title be used more rather than less prior to purchase.

books included in the record load can be imposed so that a user cannot automatically purchase, for example, any title priced over a certain dollar amount. Another option is to have either high-cost books or all purchases mediated through the library. In this situation, a staff member would review either expensive titles or conceivably all titles to determine if they should be acquired for the library. Rarely have libraries chosen to implement review of all orders placed through a PDA program, as the cost to the institution in staff time would eliminate any savings seen in time saved in the selection process. Finally, the profile of titles included in a PDA record load can be limited by publisher, publishing year, price, subject, and various other factors in order to ensure that any title purchased would support the mission of the institution. Despite the higher cost per title for those books purchased through a PDA program, the true benefit is that each title acquired has already been used.

Finding the Money

Generally speaking, the primary question librarians face when purchasing new formats is "Where is the money coming from?" For libraries with flat or declining budgets, funds for e-books will not be new money but will be money earmarked for other purchases that will have to be shifted to cover these new costs. Some collection development policies are being rewritten to assume that the collection priority is electronic, which suggests that print book budgets will be reallocated to cover the costs of the same content in electronic format. But this solution is not a panacea, as the manner in which an e-book is acquired has an impact on budget planning. Purchasing an e-book outright generally results in higher costs, as the price does not include the same discounts given to print purchasing through a book jobber. If the library determines that multiple simultaneous users are needed, the e-book can cost 50 percent more than the print version. If that same electronic title is leased, the initial annual cost may be lower than the print, but realize that there will be ongoing expenditures for each year that the title is leased. Thus, it is impossible to say that the same funds previously earmarked for print books would pay for the same number of electronic titles. On the flip side, moving to e-books can result in actual savings, but those savings are not found within the collections budget. Studies have shown that the purchase cost of a book over its lifetime is just a small percentage of its overall cost to the institution (Lawrence, Connaway, and Brigham, 2001). The additional costs include labeling, shelving, circulating, binding and other preservation activities, and overhead related to the physical plant. None of these costs is a factor in the management of an electronic book. If a patron-driven model is implemented, the costs of selection and ordering are also reduced, if not eliminated.

Finally, leasing e-books title-by-title is not the only model that results in the need for continuing money to pay for what was a one-time expense. As was discussed previously, e-books can be leased (not owned) and/or part of a subject collection that incurs annual changes. These continuing charges can be for the book itself, platform fees, or concurrent user fees. Money needed to pay for this type of resource must be continuing funds rather than one-time money, which is traditionally used for book purchases. For some libraries, where money that is guaranteed to be available every year is managed in a serials budget, and "soft" or unguaranteed funds are managed in a monographic budget, this means that monographic or book content would have to be paid out of a serials budget. With all of the other pressures placed on our serials funds, such as print serials, electronic serials packages, and databases, adding books to this group could deplete the availability of funds for other ongoing resources. One way to address this is to shift monographic funds to serials budgets but only when you are guaranteed to receive that money in subsequent years. Or, you could ask the information provider to bill you for multiple years at a time, and use monographic funds to pay that invoice. Finally, you may choose to cancel other resources, such as print serial subscriptions, to fund a new e-book database product, which would require tough decisions on the part of your collections staff.

Conclusion

The different ways in which e-book content is made available, the publication schedule of e-books and their print counterparts, as well as the availability of demand-driven acquisition purchasing all play a role in how a library budgets for e-resources. One major challenge is finding the additional ongoing funds to subscribe to e-book content when that content is made available only as part of a subscription database or a leased purchasing model. Another challenge is the potential for duplication of content in both print and electronic formats in an era when few libraries can afford to pay twice for the same book. Finally, even if e-books are purchased on a title-by-title basis using monographic funds, the cost of each individual title will be more than its print counterpart, as discounts through jobbers are not available and paperback equivalents are not an option. But, despite e-books under some circumstances being more expensive than their print counterparts, greater benefits in convenience, accessibility, increased usage, and security against loss or theft may be seen. There are still times when, for budgetary reasons, obtaining the print version of a book remains the most prudent option, although print books come with their own storage and management costs attached. E-book acquisitions are complicated, because they tend to be more expensive than print, with some ongoing charges mimicking serials collections and other hidden usage and platform expenses. As electronic resources take a larger share of collection budgets, it is important to understand all the factors and issues involved in e-book selection and licensing. In the final analysis, the library budget can be adjusted to meet the needs of library users whether that need is met by print, electronic, or a combination of both.

References

Lawrence, S.R., L.S. Connaway, and K.H. Brigham. 2001. "Life Cycle Costs of Library Collections: Creation of Effective Performance and Cost Metrics for Library Resources." *College & Research Libraries* 62, no. 6: 541–553.

Sharp, Steve, and Sarah Thompson. 2010. "'Just in Case' vs. 'Just in Time': E-Book Purchasing Models." *Serials* 23, no. 3: 201–206. *Library, Information Science & Technology Abstracts*, EBSCO*host*. Accessed November 9, 2011.

Wicht, Heather. 2005. "Selecting and Acquiring eBooks: So Many Choices, So Many Processes." *Against the Grain* 17, no. 1: 26–30. *Library, Information Science & Technology Abstracts*, EBSCO*host*. Accessed November 9, 2011.

Cataloging, Locating, and Accessing E-Books

Betsy Eggleston

Introduction

E-books are like any other library asset: they won't be used if no one can find them. And by all means, you want your users to be able to find them, both to enhance public relations by showing that the library is responsive to the changes in the way users are reading and to make the most of the library's investment. Choosing the best way to keep the e-books you have in front of your users takes some careful planning. There are a number of decisions to make as you set out that will make it easier and faster to develop finding tools and to keep them up-to-date as your holdings change over time. This chapter discusses these decisions and presents some options to consider. It also looks at the MARC record and loading record sets into the library catalog. The focus is on commercially available e-books that are either network hosted or web hosted, including those that libraries make available on e-book readers.

To Catalog or Not to Catalog

The first question to address is whether or not to include e-books in your catalog. Consider that the library catalog serves three main purposes:

1. It is an inventory of the library's assets.
2. It lets users know what library resources are available to them.
3. It provides information on how to access those resources.

A list of titles on a webpage can also serve these purposes, and many of today's library patrons are more familiar with finding what they want on a webpage than they are with using a library catalog. For them, a well-designed webpage that presents all electronically available titles either alphabetically or in useful categories will provide the quickest and easiest access. Adding a search box to the page makes a larger collection easier to navigate. A Netflix or Amazon.com user will be instantly at home and reading on his iPad in no time. Some vendors such as OverDrive will even create and host such a page and customize it so that it is consistent with the library's own webpages. Libraries can also list all of their vendors on their webpages with direct links to the vendors' catalogs. It helps if the vendor is capable of displaying only the titles that users have access to.

These solutions work well for public and school libraries with limited cataloging resources by eliminating the need to manage records in the local catalog in conjunction with changes in availability, ensuring that the patrons will have immediate access to new titles and won't be frustrated by out-of-date links to those that the vendor has withdrawn. On the other hand, most current integrated library systems (ILSs) provide a number of extended services that enhance the three basic requirements, such as acquisitions and financial tracking modules, circulation modules, and sophisticated end-user search engines.

The following questions will guide your decision whether or not to put the effort into full, title-by-title cataloging:

- Do you need to use a catalog-linked acquisition system for financial management?
- Are you planning to use your library's circulation system to manage e-book usage?
- Are you circulating single titles or an e-reader with several titles loaded on it?
- Do you want to integrate e-book discovery with that of other resources available to your users?
- Do you want to provide them with multiple access points and other searching options?

A research library with a budget divided among many separate funds, using multiple vendors with different access requirements will have a strong case for integration of e-books into the same system that it uses for its other resources. A public library with a package of leisure reading titles from a single vendor may find that its needs are entirely met without doing so.

Of course, the choices aren't mutually exclusive. Many libraries both include e-books in the library catalog and highlight them on a special webpage. The wiki Website Design (http://www.libsuccess.org/index.php?title=Website_Design) offers links to many resources that can help. It focuses on library websites and provides links to a number of well-designed library pages, both academic and public, that users have identified for the "Library Website Hall of Fame." It also includes links to a list of best books on the subject, usability and accessibility sites, and related web tools.

Factors Involving Acquisitions Records

If you use your ILS to track other acquisitions, you will want to consider including e-book purchases in that system in order to allow you to manage all of your collections budget in the same place and to facilitate accurate fund accounting. If your system requires a bibliographic record in order to build an acquisitions record, the bibliographic units that the records describe will vary depending on how the e-books or packages of e-books are paid for. For title-by-title purchases, standard cataloging records are usually ideal. If payment will not be broken down by title, a set record, similar to a record you might use for a standing order, will be needed, although you may have to improvise a title for some packages if the only unifying feature is that the books in it are all available from one vendor. If all of your purchases are of the latter type, using acquisitions records for packages in the ILS does not necessarily mean that you will need to include records for individual titles in your catalog.

Alternatively, an electronic resource management (ERM) system that includes financial data will allow you to manage an e-book budget while keeping track of usage statistics, managing links, recording license details, and providing an A–Z title list. Many also have preselected sets of MARC records that can be loaded into the library catalog and managed via largely automated processes. For more information about ERMs, see the E-Books in Practice section, Example 5, "E-Book Access Management Using an ERM System—Oregon Health & Science University."

E-books that will be available on circulating e-readers, such as Nooks, Kindles, or Sony Readers, are in a category of their own. The current model for purchasing such books for e-readers generally involves setting up an account with the vendor and storing credit card information on the vendor's site in order to allow the owner to easily purchase new books. Each title that is purchased from the e-bookstore has its own price, and thus the receipts are broken out title-by-title, allowing you to charge them to different funds if desired. Most libraries, however, make several titles available on each reader. Because the circulating unit here is the e-reader, a choice must be made whether to link purchases to the bibliographic records for individual titles or to a record for the device itself. In these relatively early days of library experience in this arena, both methods have been used, the former requiring individual cataloging records that are likely to be available either from the vendor or from a shared cataloging source such as OCLC, the latter requiring a record only for the device with added entries for the titles loaded on it, which will usually need to be created separately for each set of books.

Factors Involving Circulation Records

The ILS circulation system normally tracks which patron has a book, when it was taken out of the library, when it is due to be returned, and how many times it has been used. If titles circulate individually and there is a requirement that the circulation record be linked to a bibliographic record, full cataloging is necessary.

E-books vary a great deal in the degree to which these features are useful, because different vendors provide titles under a variety of licenses that may or may not include the concept of circulation. One vendor that uses the circulation model is OverDrive. For its e-books, however, the loan is tracked within the vendor's site, shutting circulation information off from the library circulation system. Instead, the company provides monthly statistics that can be integrated with circulation statistics from the ILS. Follett advertises that you can manage e-book circulation using the library's own circulation system. For e-books loaded on e-readers, circulation records will be required at least for the e-reader itself. If individual titles are cataloged, you will also want to link their records to that of the device, if possible, in order to provide current information on the availability of the titles loaded on it. The circulation statistics that result are those for the reader itself, with no meaningful information available for individual titles, making it impossible to ascertain, which, if any, prompted the user to check out the e-reader.

Other vendors with whom the library has a site license or a concurrent user license that is not based on a circulation model provide monthly statistics of full-text downloads and page views by content type. For these, the ILS circulation functions are unnecessary, and the choice of cataloging remains open.

Many libraries that do lend e-books in a way that mimics print circulation would like to regain control over their investments in electronic materials and be able to manage e-book lending in local systems (Kelley, 2011; OITP Task Force on E-Books, 2011). If this model becomes more prevalent, circulation systems may be more of a consideration than they are now with the advantage that circulation statistics can be gathered along with print circulation statistics. Combined with any financial information in the system, this can be a powerful tool for collection development and is a strong impetus for making the resources available for title-by-title cataloging.

Factors Associated with Integrated Searching

Librarians and teachers hope that students will take advantage of all of the materials in the library to do their research. For this reason alone, integrating all library offerings in one catalog and providing standard cataloging for each piece is worthwhile. On the other hand, when library users are looking for reading material at 2:00 a.m., they may well want a separate list of books they can download and read immediately. Whether to use a separate website for e-books, the library catalog, or a combination of both will depend on the clientele and library resources.

Evaluating Resources Needed for Cataloging

Determining the resources it will take to catalog e-books depends, to some extent, on the acquisitions model. Table 8.1 lists the problems you may encounter and the questions that will need to be asked that will help determine whether or not you have the staff time to manage e-books effectively.

Here, the problems to consider listed in Table 8.1 are broken out with some further explanation of the problem:

Table 8.1. Factors Affecting Cataloging, by Acquisitions Model

Acquisitions Model	Problems to Consider	Questions to Ask	Acquisitions/ Circulation Structures Needed
Free; web hosted	Stability of content	How will you check continued availability?	None
Package; individual titles chosen by library; subscription model; new editions added automatically	Availability of appropriate record sets; updating records as new editions come out	How will you find out when editions have been updated?	Annual payment record; budget encumbrances; vendor information record
Package; individual titles chosen by library; each edition purchased separately; perpetual access model	Availability of appropriate record sets	How is perpetual access ensured?	Payment record; vendor information record
Aggregator package; vendor chooses titles; library pays a flat annual fee	Availability of records from vendor; title stability	How will you keep records up-to-date as vendor removes and adds titles to the package?	Annual payment record; budget encumbrances; vendor information record
Paid downloadable files; must be hosted on local system	Content storage; user access; licensing: single user or site-wide access	Will the titles be a temporary or permanent part of the library's collection? What kind of electronic preservation tools are available? Does the file need to be password protected?	Record of payment
Collection of titles on e-reader	Cataloging model; physical processing and security; amount of original cataloging required	Is patron use motivated by interest in the books or the device? Will content change over time?	Record of payment; vendor record; circulation record
Individual titles on CD-ROM	Physical processing and security; format updating	What kind of classification will you use?	Record of payment; circulation record
Collection of titles on CD-ROM	Physical processing and security; format updating	Should the individual titles, the device, or the collection be cataloged?	Record of payment; circulation record
Single purchase; web hosted	Cataloging work flow	How can you ensure that non-physical e-books are not forgotten in the cataloging backlog?	Record of payment

- **Stability of content:** It is not unusual for websites and their contents to change, move, or disappear altogether over time. One day you might find a report that you want your users to be able to access through your catalog, and a year later the link will either be broken or take you to entirely different content. This occurs on government sites, academic sites, and even commercial sites. It can be the result of a change in servers, platforms, focus of the site, moving outdated information to an archive, or personnel changes. Link checkers can be helpful in identifying broken links but not in finding those whose content has changed. Keeping links up-to-date, especially for free e-books, requires a time commitment on the part of library staff. There is a strong temptation to hand over responsibility to the user to notify staff that there is a problem of this sort, but users who encounter too many of these broken links will soon lose confidence in the catalog.

- **Availability of appropriate record sets:** Many e-book vendors offer to supply MARC records with their collections. If the collection will not change over time, a set of records loaded at the time of purchase can be straightforward as long as the records follow the standards that are in place in the catalog. If the collection is likely to change in any way over time, records will need to be updated. It is important to work with the vendor to negotiate for notification and an updated record set when this happens. E-book packages that supply reference works, textbooks, or manuals, for example, are sometimes available on a subscription basis that guarantees availability of the latest edition. If the individual titles in the package are cataloged separately using standard cataloging rules, those that do not have a regular updating pattern will be cataloged on records for a specific edition. Vendors should maintain an up-to-date record set that can be loaded in the catalog whenever there are changes. Similarly, packages that continue to add new titles should supply new records whenever a new title becomes available. If such record sets are not available, the vendor should at least notify the library of changes so that updates can be made in-house.

- **Ensuring perpetual access:** At this point there really is no assurance of perpetual access to e-books. Even for those loaded on e-book readers, chances are good that the technology will soon move on, antiquating them within our lifetimes. The best that we can hope for is that the vendor will have an agreement with a trusted archive, such as Portico, that will agree to host the content and supply it to users in case the publisher or vendor goes out of business. For research libraries that are committed to maintaining a record of scholarship, this is a major consideration. Other libraries may assume a shorter information life span. They will keep the book only as long as it is of high interest to the users, and thus perpetual access is not an issue. No matter which approach your library uses, there should be a plan in place either to archive or to remove records from the catalog, both one-by-one and as part of a batch process if perpetual access fails.

- **Content storage and user access:** Those e-books that are available only for purchase as a one-time download of a PDF present a particular set of issues for libraries:

- ○ Where should they be stored?
- ○ How can they be made available to users?
- ○ How can access restrictions be applied?
- ○ How can they be preserved through format generations?

For vendor-hosted e-books, librarians have assumed that those problems are the responsibility of the vendor. For these PDFs, however, it is up to the librarian to make all of the arrangements. One inelegant solution is to print them out, put them in a binder on the shelf, and catalog them as a print reproduction of the e-book. Another solution might be to load them on a single computer in the library and note the location of the computer in lieu of a call number. If the library has access to secure archival storage space on a server, the most useful solution will be to make them available there and catalog them as you would any other e-book, depending on the copyright or license restrictions that may apply.

- **Cataloging work flow:** With print material the cataloging work flow was driven by the need to move books off the cataloger's desk and onto the shelves in the stacks. The cataloger knew that there were more books to be processed, because they appeared on the backlog shelf or in a pile on her desk. It was obvious that the books had been cataloged because they were no longer shelved in the backlog or on the cataloger's desk. The motivation to finish the work was a desire to get rid of that pile.

  E-books require a different type of notification, organization in the cataloging process, and motivation for the cataloger. For anyone purchasing occasional single titles that will need to be cataloged separately, it is important to plan and document the framework for moving them from the purchasing stage to the virtual cataloging stream, onto the cataloger's virtual desk, off the virtual desk, and into the virtual stacks. It is easy for an invisible item to become lost somewhere in that process. An e-mail message as notification from the selector to acquisitions and then to the cataloger is one way to move the process forward. Forwarding that e-mail back to the selector at the end will also provide a check to confirm that work is complete. Another way to track the e-book through the work flow would be to use a spreadsheet of new titles to be cataloged, located on a shared computer space, with columns to indicate where in the process it is. The motivation will vary from library to library.

In addition to difficulties arising from the various purchase models, a major consideration in evaluating whether there are sufficient resources to maintain e-books in the catalog is whether your ILS provides tools for batch loading and unloading records. If your catalog does not support batch record loads and does not have mechanisms to remove record sets based on information in the records, cataloging e-books in a package of any size will require significant staff time. Finding and deleting out-of-date records will take more time. Thus, deciding whether it is worth adding records to the catalog will depend on how many you are likely to offer.

Other useful tools you might hope to find in your ILS are uniform resource locator (URL) checkers (or link checkers, designed to attempt to locate a website using its address [URL] and produce a list of addresses that send back errors so that staff can check and correct them); loading programs that allow staff to add, delete, or replace record fields and text in batch mode; and duplicate detection and overlay capability.

In the end, the decision to fully catalog e-books boils down to whether you have the resources available to maintain an accurate catalog of your offerings. If so, including each title in the library catalog, complete with subject headings, classification, and personal and corporate headings will be the best way to get the maximum advantage for the money that you've spent. It will also go the furthest toward meeting the needs of your users.

Making E-Books Available to Users

If, after considering the alternatives, you make the decision to include e-books in your catalog, you will need to plan how to construct the records to provide the best access to them. The planning should include an implementation of license restrictions, including user authentication and restriction, URL management, whether or not to use the "single-record" approach, when collection-level records will suffice, how to use vendor record sets, cataloging conventions and standards, and, finally, rules for constructing the MARC record itself. This section focuses on those issues that are important in planning a cataloging policy that will result in up-to-date and reliable access for your users.

Dealing with License Restrictions

A large proportion of the web-hosted e-books available to libraries today are governed by license agreements between the library and the vendor. These were addressed in an earlier chapter. Almost all of these licenses require that the library provide some kind of mechanism to limit uses to those specified in the license. In some cases the vendor will do that for you. In providing access to your e-book collections you must remember to make provisions for following the terms of the license. If the license restricts usage to an IP address or range of IP addresses (IP, or Internet protocol, addresses identify computers on a network; an IP range identifies a group of computers on that network), the vendor will take care of enforcing the restriction by allowing access only to the resources that have been licensed to requests that are made from the IP address specified in the license. Generally, this will mean that the book is available only on computers in the library or in a group of buildings in a certain limited geographic location. The usage can, however, be extended to remote users if they have a way of connecting to the IP range through VPN or similar software (e.g., via a proxy server). VPN, or virtual private network, is a network that allows access to an organization's IP ranges to remote users. Many universities use this to allow their faculty, staff, and students to use internal resources while traveling or working from home. For any resources where the license restriction is dependent on user IDs or passwords, some mechanism must be in place to authenticate users. Some publisher sites provide log-in screens that accommodate individual subscribers and institutions using the Athens log-in or an institutional log-in. In these cases, again, the problem of distributing log-in information to users is not necessarily a cataloging issue.

Using Proxy Servers

Most U.S. institutions rely on a proxy server to mediate requests for remotely hosted material. The proxy server uses certain filters to evaluate requests and, if it determines that the request is valid, provides a connection to the remote server. The proxy server may validate the user by the IP address of the incoming request, or it may depend on an authorization protocol based on a database of the institution's personnel, students, or library card holders. In this case, the cataloger must remember to use a specially formulated URL that will route the request from the catalog to the book through the library's proxy server. In this case, the URLs provided by the vendor will need to be modified before they are entered in the catalog. The modification will vary depending on the proxy server and the institution.

Managing URLs

You may also want to consider what means you wish to employ to help you keep your URLs in the catalog up-to-date. Although there are not as many problems now as there once were with resources changing addresses, rendering your carefully crafted records useless to your patrons, it still happens. When a large publisher changes platform, thousands of URLs will change, and, if the publisher has not sent a file of updated links, all of your records for that vendor's titles will be affected. Rather than changing those links one-by-one in the catalog, thought should be given to providing persistent identifiers that will redirect traffic from an old URL to a more recent one or including name resolution software that will also allow for the seamless redirection of links that have changed in a far more efficient work flow.

Records for E-Books in the Library Catalog

Once the decision has been made to include bibliographic records in the library catalog, other decisions regarding the questions listed here will need to follow:

- Should you use a single record for print and electronic versions or multiple records?
- When is a collection-level record appropriate rather than individual records?

- Will you use vendor-supplied records, OCLC collection sets, ERM-supplied records, or records created in-house? How will you facilitate batch loading of e-books?
- How will you facilitate batch loading of vendor-supplied records?
- Will you use provider-neutral records in your local catalog?

Single versus Multiple Records for Electronic Version and Print Version

The question of multiple versions first arose when libraries were cataloging microform reproductions. At the time it seemed like a good idea to use a single record: many microfilms were reproductions of books or journals that the library held, and adding holdings information to the record for the print title to show that the library also had a microform reproduction was far less time-consuming than making separate records for each. It also kept the catalog indexes more straightforward for the user by limiting the number of records to choose from.

As new formats appeared, libraries that had made the decision to use a single record for different formats have begun to reconsider their decision. The IFLA Study Group's (1998) *Functional Requirements for Bibliographic Records* (FRBR) report, which promulgates a philosophic framework for the presentation of information, and the subsequent involvement of ILS vendors in implementing such a presentation have raised questions about whether the algorithms for sorting records will work if the single-record approach is being used. Furthermore, electronic books and journals have required more complicated and often unsatisfactory decisions over the years, from developing a mechanism to separate the versions when sharing records with systems that use the separate record approach to dealing with the inconsistency of some e-books being described on records for print books and others being described on records for the e-book when the library does not own the print copy.

Unfortunately, the standards are blurry. *Anglo-American Cataloguing Rules*, Second Edition, focuses on "bring[ing] out all aspects of the item being described, including its content [and] its carrier [physical form]" (Joint Steering Committee for Revision of AACR, 2005; AACR2 Rule 0.24), implying an endorsement of the use of separate records. Separate records are preferred in OCLC: "Creating separate records for an item is preferable when both remote and directly tangible (non-remote) versions exist" (OCLC, 2011; Section 3.9), and the Library of Congress uses separate records in its catalog. On the other hand, the Program for Cooperative Cataloging (PCC) documentation allows either option.

Here are some of the benefits of using a single record:

- When you are cataloging manually, it is easier to add a holdings record linked to a bibliographic record for a print version that is already in the catalog.

- In catalogs that can load records with duplicate detection and overlay, poor cataloging in vendor-supplied e-book records can be discarded when a record for the print version is available.
- Users can see all formats available to them by opening only one record.
- Coding for the e-book can be stored in a holdings record.

The multiple-version approach also has its advantages:

- Loading and unloading vendor record sets can be done without having a mechanism to find and merge print records.
- No coding is lost in a catalog that does not support holdings records.
- No special programming is needed to share records.
- Catalog index displays can show users immediately which record is the record for the e-book.
- Separate records provide a more consistent display for e-books.

Whichever option you choose, remember that coding for the electronic version must be available in order to facilitate catalog displays highlighting electronically available materials.

Furthermore, records referring to books in a vendor package should contain coding to facilitate removing the records in a batch process, even if the library's current system does not support such a process. The coding should also facilitate duplication detection and resolution in batch replacement of records for sets that have changed and require an updated record set.

SINGLE-RECORD APPROACH: MARC BIBLIOGRAPHIC RECORD FOR PRINT TITLE	
LDR	cam a2200433 a 4500
001	012099681-2
008	081020s2010 nyua b 001 0 eng
010	$a 2008044963
016 7	$a 101487030 $2 DNLM
020	$a 9780071547697 (set : alk. paper)
020	$a 007154769X (set : alk. paper)
020	$a 9780071547703 (hardcover : alk. paper)
020	$a 0071547703 (hardcover : alk. paper)
020	$a 9780071547710 (DVD)
020	$a 0071547711 (DVD)
	(Continued)

SINGLE-RECORD APPROACH: MARC BIBLIOGRAPHIC RECORD FOR PRINT TITLE *(Continued)*	
035 0	$a ocn263295031
040	$a DNLM/DLC $c DLC $d NLM $d YDXCP $d BTCTA $d C#P
042	$a pcc
050 00	$a RD31 $b .P88 2010
060 10	$a WO 100 $b S399 2010
082 00	$a 617 $2 22
245 00	$a Schwartz's principles of surgery / $c editor-in-chief, F. Charles Brunicardi; associate editors, Dana K. Andersen . . . [et al.].
246 30	$a Principles of surgery
250	$a 9th ed.
260	$a New York : $b McGraw-Hill, Medical Pub. Division, $c c2010.
300	$a xxi, 1866 p. : $b ill. (chiefly col.) ; $c 29 cm. + $e 1 DVD (4 3/4 in.)
500	$a DVD-ROM in pocket.
504	$a Includes bibliographical references and index.
538	$a System requirements: DVD-ROM drive.
655 0	$a Electronic books.
650 0	$a Surgery.
650 12	$a General Surgery.
650 22	$a Surgical Procedures, Operative.
700 1	$a Schwartz, Seymour I., $d 1928-
700 1	$a Brunicardi, F. Charles.

MARC HOLDINGS RECORD FOR E-BOOK	
001	017178891
005	20091019095022.0
007	cr|???|||||||
008	0904202u 8 4001uu 0000000
506	$a This resource may be restricted to users with a valid Harvard ID
852	$b NET $c ACMED
856 4	$u http://nrs.harvard.edu/urn-3:hul.e-book:ACCESS_0071446877

MARC HOLDINGS RECORD FOR PRINT BOOK	
001	107693358
005	20100331153101.0
007	vd|uvuizu
008	1003232g 8 4001uu 0000000
079 0	$a ocn263295031
079 2	$a ocn589578659
852	$b MED $c GEN $z Currently in Reserve $h WO 100 $i S399 2010 $z Includes 1 disc in pocket
854 00	$8 1 $a (unit)
864 41	$8 1.1 $a Text
864 41	$8 1.2 $a 1 DVD-ROM

One cautionary note: some electronic versions of print titles are so different that they will need separate records in any case. This is especially true of online continually updating versions of print books. In the sidebars (pp. 108–109) there are examples of records for the print and the online versions of *Metabolic & Molecular Bases of Inherited Disease*. In this case the online version is continually updated, and the content has diverged considerably from that of the printed four-volume set published in 2001. Even though the policy at this library is to use a single record for print and electronic works, the records are separated. Notice that the online version is coded "ai" in the seventh and eighth positions of the LDR and that the date in the 260 field is open, while the print version is coded "am" and the date is closed. Cataloging the resources separately also allowed the cataloger to more easily express other differences between the versions, including the variation in title. There will be further discussion of these differences in the later section MARC Standards for Cataloging E-Books.

Collection-Level Records

When libraries don't have the resources to put in to fully cataloging a group of materials and a vendor-supplied record set is not an option, one fallback position is to use a collection-level record to describe the set. The bibliographic unit in this record is not the individual title but the set itself, for example, Springer Protocols, Intelex Past Masters, The American Civil War: Letters and Diaries. The record gives no details about the titles that are included but includes a URL that will take the users to the database homepage where they can choose the title they want. For well-known e-book collections, especially those in which the individual titles are not distinctive or are less important than the collection, this may be all that is really

RECORD FOR AN ONLINE UPDATING RESOURCE	
LDR	^^^^^nai^^2200349la^4500
001	011575927-1
005	20110303094749.0
006	m^^^^^^^^d^^^^^^^
008	061117c20019999nyu^x^d^s^^^^^0^^^^2eng^d
035 0	$a ocm76292642
040	$a LML $c LML
090	$a RC627.8 $b .S37
245 00	$a Scriver's OMMBID$h[electronic resource] : $b the online metabolic & molecular bases of inherited disease / $c Scriver ... [et al.].
246 30	$a OMMBID
246 3	$a Online metabolic & molecular bases of inherited disease
246 3	$a Metabolic and molecular bases of inherited disease
260	$a [New York] : $b McGraw-Hill, $c c2001-
300	$a 1 online resource
538	$a Mode of access: Internet via the World Wide Web.
500	$a Title from home page (viewed Nov. 17, 2006).
500	$a Online version of: The metabolic & molecular bases of inherited disease / editors, Charles R. Scriver ... [et al.].
520	$a "Online access to a compendium of genetic disorders and information from the entire field of genetics ... Obtain answers as well as retrieve updates on pathophysiology and treatment"—About page.
650 0	$a Metabolism, Inborn errors of.
650 0	$a Pathology, Molecular.
650 0	$a Genetic disorders.
650 0	$a Genetics.
650 12	$a Genetic Diseases, Inborn.
650 22	$a Metabolic Diseases.
650 22	$a Metabolism, Inborn Errors.
655 7	$a Electronic books. $2 local
700 1	$a Scriver, Charles R.
730 0	$a Metabolic & molecular bases of inherited disease.

EXAMPLE OF PRINT MONOGRAPH	
LDR	00925cam^^22002898a^4500
001	008530419-0
005	20080929120651.0
008	000725s2001^^^^nyuaf^^^^b^^^^001^0^eng^c
010	$a ^^^00060957^
016 7	$a 100960823$2DNLM
020	$a 0079130356 (set)
035 0	$a ocm44678633
040	$a NLM $c NLM $d OCL $d HMS
042	$a pcc
050 00	$a RC627.8 $b .M47 2001
060 10	$a WD 200 $b M5865 2001
245 04	$a The metabolic & molecular bases of inherited disease / $c editors, Charles R. Scriver ... [et al.].
246 3	$a Metabolic and molecular bases of inherited disease
250	$a 8th ed.
260	$a New York : $b McGraw-Hill, $c c2001.
300	$a 4 v., [12] p. of col. plates : $b ill. ; $c 29 cm.
504	$a Includes bibliographical references and index.
650 12	$a Genetic Diseases, Inborn.
650 22	$a Metabolic Diseases.
650 22	$a Metabolism, Inborn Errors.
700 1	$a Scriver, Charles R.

necessary. In most cases, however, the collection-level record is considered a "stop-gap" measure, good enough until there is time to do a thorough job.

See the example of a collection-level record in the sidebar (p. 110). Although each of the diaries has an author and could be cataloged on its own record, the library has chosen to make one record to encompass the whole collection, presumably on the understanding that patrons would be interested in the collection more for the sake of its significance to the time period than because of a particular interest in one of the authors.

MARC RECORD FOR A COLLECTION OF DIARIES AND LETTERS	
LDR	nam a
001	001937997
008	00000m20019999vau ob 000 0deng d
006	m d
007	c $b r $d m $e n $f u
043	n-us---
245 00	American Civil War $h [electronic resource] : $b letters and diaries.
260	Alexandria, VA : $b Alexander Street Press, $c c2001-
500	Title from home page (viewed Aug. 28, 2001).
538	Mode of Access: World Wide Web.
504	Includes bibliographical references.
520	Access to more than 400 sources of diaries, letters, and memoirs written by the famous and the unknown politicians, generals, slaves, landowners, seaman, wives, and spies, providing the Northern, Southern and foreign perspectives. Materials can be searched by author, subject, date, battle, and material type.
651 0	United States $x History $y Civil War, 1861-1865 $v Personal narratives.

Record Sets from Vendors

There are often at least three routes to adding e-books to the library catalog: loading records provided by the e-book vendor, using OCLC WorldCat or another library vendor's prepared collection sets, or doing the cataloging in-house. When you are working with collections of hundreds or even thousands of e-book titles that the vendor may add to or delete from at any time, an accurate set of records that can easily be loaded into your catalog when you buy the set and can be replaced when the set changes can make an enormous difference in the feasibility of providing individual records in the catalog as opposed to listing the package on your webpage and expecting your users to explore it in the hopes of finding what they want.

Many vendors offer to provide MARC records with e-book purchases. The quality of these records varies according to whether they were created by untrained staff or by well-seasoned catalogers. It is advisable to request a large sample set in order to evaluate the records even before the purchase is complete so that you will have a chance to negotiate for better records if the ones on offer are not sufficient. In conjunction with this step, the library should prepare specifications for acceptable records. The combined effect of libraries working with vendors to ensure quality records will, in the end, save time for patrons and catalogers everywhere.

Remember: the more complete and accurate the data and coding in records is, the more it will be possible to do with them. Making use of faceted displays, FRBR-ized catalogs, and analytic reports from the catalog is easiest if the data in these records is consistent with that in the rest of the catalog. Naturally, the temptation to ignore the quality of the records is strong when you have purchased a large package, but taking the time to make an informed decision and to consider the ramifications of using nonstandard records is worthwhile.

A good many articles have been published recently about the problems of loading vendor-supplied records for e-books. Martin and Mundle (2010) cite three categories of problems that they have found in vendor records for e-books: those that interfere with loading records in the catalog, those that prevent users from finding the records, and those that diminish the quality of data. These are some of the problems that they found when they first tried to load vendor-supplied records for a Springer e-book package:

- Records contained improperly formed or ambiguous ISBNs and other standard numbers that had the potential to cause duplicate detection and overlay problems during the batch loading process.
- Some URLs were broken or missing.
- The vendor did not supply records for all books in the package and included some records for titles that were not in the contract.
- Records contained encoding problems, especially those for books in German.
- Nonauthoritative forms of access points had been used.
- Analysis of multivolume sets was inconsistent.

Working with the vendor to upgrade the records solved many of the problems, but not all.

Sanchez and Rentz (2011: 14) recommend using the following required criteria for accepting a vendor's record set:

- Accurate title
- Accurate edition
- Author
- Title-level URL
- MARC formatting is correct for use in your ILS

They also list the following considerations/questions to ask about the record set, all of which will inform you in making the decision regarding the efficiency of using them:

- Source of the records should be known
- Treatment of reproductions, sets and serials should be known
- Will smaller bibliographic units, i.e., volumes, abstracts, chapters, poems, etc., be included?
- Have access points been subjected to authority control?

- Can the vendor edit to the library's specifications, including local additions, or is there a charge?

- Is there a unique 001, and where does it come from and how is it formatted?

- Has the e-book cataloging set been deduped? [i.e., have duplicates been removed?]

- Do records match the content purchased—is there an e-resource for each record and vice-versa?

- Is your system's record loading functionality capable of handling the records and what tweaks might be needed?

- Will records be delivered in a timely manner as soon as the e-resources are available? (Sanchez and Rentz, 2011: 17)

The question of who owns the records and whether you are allowed to share them in any way is also important to clarify. Any records that the vendor does not allow you to share should be flagged so that any automated export programs will omit them.

The Library of Congress and the PCC have recently updated the *MARC Record Guide for Monograph Aggregator Vendors* (Culbertson et al., 2009) to provide vendors minimum standards for the records that they supply to libraries. You can use this document both to evaluate record sets and to inform your vendors of the kind of records you need.

There are ways to improve record sets that consistently misuse codes or include extraneous fields. If your ILS record loader has a feature that allows the importer to make the same changes to all of the records that are coming into the catalog, you can use that to add fields that you need and remove subfields that you don't want. If the records contain added entries for the vendor, unwanted text in the URL field, or vendor-specific notes, for example, you can prevent those from loading by creating, or asking your systems librarian to create, a loader table that excludes them.

Another tool that is used widely to make changes to record sets is MarcEdit. This software, created by Terry Reese, a librarian and former cataloger at Oregon State University, is a free MARC editing platform that can be downloaded from Reese's website (http://people.oregonstate.edu/~reeset/marcedit/html/index.php). It also includes "a full suite of XML related tools specific to the library community" (Reese, 2011). MarcEdit can add fields, delete fields, modify subfields, perform conditional changes, translate from XML to MARC and back again, add records through a Z39.50 interface, translate character encoding, and much more. Furthermore, it can export records to an ILS through an interface that is very like the OCLC gateway export. In short, it can solve many problems with record sets. The MarcEdit website contains numerous help features, including a feedback box that allows you to request help from the programmer himself.

Reese and others have also published "how to" guides on the web and YouTube videos explaining how to take advantage of specific functions (Reese, 2009). Titles include "MarcEdit Basics," "MarcEdit's MarcBreaker," and "Managing Plug-Ins Using the MarcEdit Plug-In Manager."

Some other idiosyncrasies that may be more difficult to address are those of nonstandard name headings, nonstandard subject headings, alternative approaches to the bibliographic unit, and serial volumes on individual records. If the vendor's record set is not going to work in the ILS and the records are impossible to rework into a form that will be consistent with the standards of your catalog, there may still be an effective alternative. In many cases, sets of records are available from OCLC's WorldCat Collection Sets or from other cataloging services. These are not free, but they are often more accurate and require much less "fixing." If the number of e-books you have purchased is large and comes with no records or unusable records, check for the availability of sets from cataloging agencies or other library services before either cataloging them one by one or adding records to your catalog that are going to create more difficulties with ongoing cataloging.

Provider-Neutral Records

The same e-book is often available from a variety of vendors on different platforms, each with its own features, possibly its own title page, series, product code, and search capabilities. Until 2009, cataloging rules required separate records for each vendor's version of what was essentially the same title. The multiplicity of records in record-sharing databases and even local catalogs became a problem for users in interpreting search results and time-consuming for catalogers who needed to produce original records for each vendor's edition. Recognizing the problem, the PCC developed and approved new guidelines for cataloging e-books that was published online as the *Provider-Neutral E-Monograph MARC Record Guide* (Culbertson, Mandelstam, and Prager, 2011). Anyone cataloging e-books should become familiar with this guide. It is written for the practicing cataloger and contains an easy-to-use field-by-field chart on how to code MARC fields and what sources to use for description. It is the current standard for cataloging e-books for record-sharing databases such as OCLC. The principles can also be applied to shared catalogs used by consortia, educational systems, and local networks.

The guide "emphasizes recording only information applicable to all manifestations with the same content" (Culbertson, Mandelstam, and Prager, 2011: 3). To overcome the problem of differences in presentation of essentially the same content on different vendor platforms, the guide-lines promote the use of cataloging based on a record for the original print edition rather than a strict transcription from the item being cata-loged. The provider-neutral record generally makes no mention of individual titles on different platforms, nor does it record reproduction information in notes except in the case of certain preservation projects.

While the guide states explicitly that "all libraries may follow whatever policies they wish in their local online public access catalogs (OPACs)" (Culbertson, Mandelstam, and Prager, 2011: 2), the most efficient course for those who use records from a large supplier is to follow similar policies in the local catalog. It can save frustration for the user and time for the cataloger. More information about the guidelines is included in the following discussion of MARC fields.

MARC Standards for Cataloging E-Books

If no acceptable records are available elsewhere, they will need to be created in-house. Both to catalog individual e-books and to evaluate records from a supplier, you need an understanding of the current standards and a sense of impending changes. The most common cataloging standards in use today in the English-speaking world are the *Anglo-American Cataloguing Rules*, Second Edition (AACR2) for description (Joint Steering Committee for Revision of AACR, 2005) paired with the *MARC21 Format for Bibliographic Data* (MARC21) for coding (Library of Congress, 2011). As early as January 2013 new rules for description will be adopted, *RDA: Resource Description and Access* (RDA) (Joint Steering Committee for Development of RDA, 2011). Rules for cataloging e-books using these standards are not very different from those for cataloging print books. In the following discussion, knowledge of standards for print book cataloging is assumed. The focus is on the differences between the two.

Bibliographic Format

MARC bibliographic formats are commonly listed using these generic but inaccurate terms: books, computer files, maps, mixed materials, music, serials, and visual materials. The formats differ in that they each rely on a slightly different structure of the fields that contain coded elements of the record. These are referred to as the "fixed fields." While some elements are common to all formats, others pertain to a specific format and code aspects of the medium. That is, serial format fixed fields contain codes for periodicity and regularity, while map format fixed fields have codes for relief and projection.

With e-books, the choice of format can be confusing. Is it a book or a computer file? If there is a print title that is updated with a new edition every few years, and the corresponding e-book is continuously updated, is it still a book, or has it become an integrating resource? Is an electronic geographic atlas a book, a computer file, or a collection of maps?

Monographic E-book Leader	LDR	^^^^^nam^^2200361^a^4500
Updating E-book Leader	LDR	^^^^^nai^^2200349^a^4500

The first field in the MARC record, the Leader, or LDR, contains 24 coding positions beginning with position 00. The codes that define the format of the record are stored in LDR 06/07 (see example above). The 06 position defines the Type of Record and is more often based on the content of the item being cataloged than on the physical carrier and thus for e-books is "*a*," language material. The 07 position, the Bibliographic Level, will be "*m*," monograph, unless the book is being updated continually, in which case the code will be "*i*" for integrating resource. These codes, which together define the format, are used whenever the object being cataloged is primarily text and it is considered complete or

AACR2 RECORD	
LDR	cam 4a
001	166332032
005	20111018085430.1
008	070827s2006 enk ob 000 0 eng c
006	m d
007	c $b r $d c $e n
040	GZM $c GZM $d Z6E
020	184369588X
020	9781843695882
042	pcc
245 00	Farmers' views on the future of food and small scale producers $h [electronic resource] : $b summary of an electronic conference, 14 April to 1 July, 2005 / $c Michel Pimbert, Khanh Tran-Thanh, Estelle Deléage [... et al.], editors.
260	London : $b IIED, $c c2006.
300	ix, 75 p. (digital file, PDF)
490 1	Reclaiming diversity and citizenship
500	Title from title screen (viewed on Aug. 27, 2007).
504	Includes bibliographical references (p. 71).
538	Mode of access: World Wide Web.
538	System requirements: Adobe Acrobat Reader.
700 1	Pimbert, Michel P.
700 1	Tran-Thanh, Khanh.
700 1	Deléage, Estelle.
710 2	International Institute for Environment and Development.
830 0	Reclaiming diversity and citizenship.
856 40	$u http://www.iied.org/pubs/pdf/full/14503IIED.pdf

is continually updated, as the case may be. That is, it is neither music nor cartographic material, nor is it a serial publication or a collection. Thus, you catalog e-books on a book format record just as you would a print monograph. An updating e-book should be cataloged on a serial format or integrating resource record as are loose-leafs that are designed to receive replacement pages. The use of the code for computer files is

PROVIDER-NEUTRAL RECORD	
LDR	cam a
001	704939648
005	20110303125126.3
008	110303s2010 dcu ol f000 0 eng c
006	m d f
007	c $b r $d b $e n
040	GPO $c GPO $d GPO
042	pcc
043	n-us---
074	0575 (online)
086 0	AE 2.110:111-341
088	Public Law 111-341
110 1	United States.
240 10	Criminal History Background Checks Pilot Extension Act of 2010
245 13	An Act to Extend the Child Safety Pilot Program $h [electronic resource].
260	[Washington, D.C. : $b U.S. G.P.O., $c 2010]
300	1 online resource ([1] leaf)
500	Title from title screen (viewed on March 3, 2011).
500	"Dec. 22, 2010 (S. 3998)."
500	"124 Stat. 3606."
500	"Public Law 111-341."
650 0	Employee screening $x Law and legislation $z United States.
776 08	$i Print version: $a United States. $t Act to Extend the Child Safety Pilot Program $w (OCoLC)704933633
856 40	$3 Text version: $u http://purl.fdlp.gov/GPO/gpo4395
856 40	$3 PDF version: $u http://purl.fdlp.gov/GPO/gpo4396

very limited, and the format documentation provides good, succinct instructions on when it is appropriate.

MARC Control Fields

There are six fixed-length control fields in a MARC record, three of which contain coded data recording certain aspects of the content and

RDA RECORD	
LDR	cam i
001	711004485
005	20110421051806.4
008	110404t20112011txu ob 000 0 eng c
006	m d
007	c $b r $d m $e n
040	STF $e rda $b eng $c STF $d UBY
042	pcc
050 14	Z701.3.C65 $b B34 2011
100 1	Bailey, Charles W. $q (Charles Wesley), $d 1950- $e compiler.
245 10	Digital curation and preservation bibliography 2010 / $c Charles W. Bailey, Jr.
260	Houston, TX : $b Digital Scholarship, $c [2011], ©2011.
300	1 online resource (76 pages) : $b PDF.
336	text $2 rdacontent
337	computer $2 rdamedia
338	online resource $2 rdacarrier
588	Viewed April 4, 2011.
650 0	Digital preservation.
650 0	Electronic publications $x Conservation and restoration.
650 0	Archival materials $x Digitization.
655 0	Electronic books.
776 08	$i Electronic reproduction of (manifestation): $a Bailey, Charles W. (Charles Wesley), 1950-. $t Digital curation and preservation bibliography 2010. $d Houston, TX : Digital Scholarship, ©2011. $h 76 pages ; 23 cm $z 9781460913321 $w (OCoLC)706727193
856 40	$u http://digital-scholarship.org/dcpb/dcpb2010.pdf
856 40	$u http://purl.stanford.edu/pk342vd9984

physical medium of an item that can be used to manipulate search results, to create reports, or to discover all of the books the library has cataloged that were published in Morocco in 1960. These are the 006, 007, and 008 fields, and they all need special attention in e-book cataloging. The other three fields are also useful in managing record loads for e-books. The 001 field contains a unique number for identifying the particular record in its native database; the 003 field, a code for that database from a standard code list. The 005 field records the date and time of the latest update to the record.

```
001   1239823098
005   20111015042730.3
008   101021s2011^^^^dcua^^^^^ob^^^^ 001^0^eng^d
006   m||||^^||d|^||||||
007   cr^bn^||||||||
```

The 008 and 006 Fields

The **008** field is a part of every MARC bibliographic record, and no record can have more than one. Each format includes two sets of codes in the 008 field, those that are common to all formats (these include the year of publication and country of publication codes) and those that are specific to a given format (for monographic language material, these include literary form, illustrations, and whether or not the piece is a biography among other things). Because only one form can be coded for here, a separate field, the 006, which includes only format-specific codes, is available for recording information for pieces with multiple format aspects (online books, video serials, online atlases, etc.).

The codes in both fields are based on information in the bibliographic record and should correspond to the text in the variable fields. Thus, on the provider-neutral record, they will reflect the information for the original that is entered in the 245, 260, and 300 fields. The only code that is specific to the electronic version of a book is in position 23 (29 in Cartographic and Visual materials formats), the Form of Item. There are three codes that may be used for e-books: **o, online; q, Direct electronic (CD-ROM, DVD, or other tangible medium); and s, electronic (can be used as a generic code)**. For most of the e-books that libraries are currently accessing, the code **o** will be appropriate.

The **006** field is used for e-material whenever the main format of the record is not the computer file format. It consists of the special coding for computer files that is not available in the 008 for book records. The first character in the 006 string defines a format. For the computer file 006, the code is **m**. In some library systems, the presence of this field is what allows the user to limit his search to both books and electronic materials. Although the field can be repeated in the record, it is not appropriate to use it on records that are also serving to describe print versions for libraries using the single-record approach. In those catalogs, it should be entered in the holdings record if available.

The 007 Field

The **007** field contains codes for aspects of the physical carrier of the item being cataloged. Like the 006 field, the first character defines the format. For e-books this will be **c**. The MARC format provides 13 other character positions following the c to record codes for the specific material, color, dimensions, whether or not the medium includes sound or there is sound on a separate medium, and various aspects of reformatting that are used by agencies involved in digital preservation. The first two characters can be used to sort result sets by physical format and are very useful in presenting faceted search results. For online books the code in the 01 position will be **r** for **remote** resource.

The 001, 003, and 005 Fields

To accurately manage loading record sets and updates into your catalog you will need to be able to identify the records precisely and to compare versions. The **001** field is the unique identifier or control number for the record in the catalog. The **003** field is a control number identifier or the code for the organization in whose database the number applies; it generally does not display in the catalog but is present in records being communicated from one system to another. Because each system has its own unique identifier entered in its 001 field, the 003 field can be programmatically merged with the 001 field on import and transferred to the 035 (MARC21: 035—System Control Number: "Control number of a system other than the one whose control number is contained in field 001"), creating a field that is unique and understood by both databases.

The **005** field is a detailed representation of the moment of the last update, accurate to the nearest one-tenth of a second. This field can be used in the process of loading updated record sets that have been supplied by vendors and batch loaded into your catalog to identify versions of the records and to limit changes to those records last updated before, after, or on a certain date.

Numbers and Codes Fields

There are other numbers that are potentially useful in identifying records. These include the ISBN, recorded in the 020 field, the 035 field, mentioned earlier, as well as the publisher number (028) and a variety of others that are often used by library systems in their duplicate detection and resolution algorithms. When the vendor sends an updated file, its system numbers can be compared to those in the 035 fields in the records in your catalog to find absolute matches that identify records to be replaced or deleted. An algorithm can also alert the system to discard an incoming record if it matches a number in one of these fields of an existing record. Because the programs that load records vary from system to system, the cataloger should be aware of their behavior in his or her local catalog. For efficiency's sake, it is, of course, best if the matching algorithm uses the numbers that will be assigned to the records in standard cataloging practice or can be assigned automatically. The 020, or ISBN field, is thus a good candidate. The ISBN (International Standard Book Number) Agency (2011) requires a separate ISBN for each file format of an e-book. The agency's online FAQ describes the distinctions that should be made: "The key features are whether any specific device or software is required to read the e-book and what user functionality is provided (e.g., copy, print, lend, etc.). As mentioned earlier, this is normally defined by a combination of file format and Digital Rights Management software" (http://www.isbn-international.org/faqs/view/17). This means that many vendors' e-books will have their own ISBNs that can be used to identify their product. The PCC guide recommends that if an e-book has been issued by multiple publishers with different ISBNs the cataloger should add each one to the provider-neutral record in a separate 020 field (Culbertson, Mandelstam, and Prager, 2011: 5). Thus the system's matching algorithm can be used to overlay individual vendor records with the single provider-neutral record if it is set up appropriately. Other record loaders may depend on the OCLC number, also entered in the 035 field, as a match point. If this is the case, you will want to ensure that the record number for the correct OCLC record, whether print or electronic, is entered there.

Classification numbers can also be useful for e-books. Although e-books don't require them in order for users to find the book in the stacks, they can be used even more effectively than subject headings to bring together virtual subject collections and to create virtual shelf browsing. Whether or not you have the facility to present collections this way now, adding a classification number will increase the possible uses of your records in the future.

Title Statement (245 Field)

Formal statement of titles, authorship, and publication details are often missing in e-books. Many do not include a title screen or a title page. The rules, however, are flexible on this point of choosing a source of information from which to record these statements in cataloging. AACR2 Rule 9.0B1 gives catalogers comparatively liberal guidelines in its definition of "chief source of information" for electronic resources, declaring it to be "the resource itself," further described as "the title screen(s), main menus, program statements, initial display(s) of information, home page(s), the file header(s) including 'Subject:' lines, encoded metadata (e.g., TEI headers, HTML/XML meta tags)." However, as mentioned earlier, if you are creating provider-neutral records the title and statement of responsibility for reproductions of print books are not transcribed from the e-book at all but rather are based on the original publication. For born-digital books, the choice of chief source of information is determined according to AACR2 rules, so it is often the title screen if there is one. The 245 field should also include a subfield **h** [**electronic resource**] following subfields **a**, **n**, and **p**, but not **b**, when the cataloger is using AACR2 rules. In RDA cataloging, the subfield **h** is no longer used. Instead, the new fields 336, 337, and 338 (see later) provide a home for the more formal and detailed machine readable details of the physical format.

Physical Description (3XX Fields)

The 300 field for online resources was not used until after 2004, when the AACR2 rules for cataloging electronic resources were revised and an optional provision was added that allowed the cataloger to include it. Recently, the Library of Congress and the PCC have reinstated it for e-books. The current standard is to use "1 online resource" in the subfield a of the 300 field, followed by the number of pages, charts, or leaves in parentheses. The dimensions of the print book are not included

AACR2 form:
    300   1 online resource (256 p.) :
        $b ill.
RDA form:
    300   1 online resource (256 pages) :
        $b illustrations

in the provider-neutral record for a digital reproduction. RDA rules result in a similar statement, with the only difference being that any abbreviations require that terms be spelled out.

Using RDA rules, the cataloger also replaces the General Material Designation, subfield h in field 245, with three 3XX fields, 336, 337, and 338, which are used for noting the content type, the media type, and the carrier type. Terms for use in these fields are supplied in lists available at the Library of Congress website (http://www.loc.gov/standards/valuelist/).

Series

In cataloging a title using the vendor-neutral record, the PCC guidelines say that for e-books that are reproductions of an original print source, use only the series that appeared on the print book; for born-digital e-books, use the series on the e-book that applies to all versions of the e-book.

Notes

Standard cataloging rules require certain notes on records. For electronic books these include the following in addition to those required for all material types:

- **System requirements/Mode of access notes:** AACR2, in Chapter 9 rev., requires the System requirements note (entered in MARC field 538) "if the information is readily available"; however, the requirement has been progressively modified as system requirements have become more standardized and as most computers have the software to read a variety of text files. In the PCC instructions for provider-neutral records, the requirement is to "Use [field 538] for records for DLF Registry of Digital Masters and other digital preservation projects." In RDA, rule 3.20.1.3 instructs the cataloger to "record any system requirements beyond what is normal and obvious for the type of carrier or type of file."

  The circumstances requiring a Mode of access note, also coded in MARC field 538, also differ depending on the rules or guidelines being used. With AACR2, the cataloger makes the note if the resource is available only by remote access. This has been completely reversed in the PCC provider-neutral document, which requires it "only if the resource is accessed by a means other than the World Wide Web" (Culbertson, Mandelstam, and Prager, 2011: 7). In RDA, while no rule requires such a note, the example of a Structured Description of the Related Manifestation for an electronic reproduction under 27.1.1.3 includes it, presumably as an optional addition.

- **Source of title proper/Basis for identification of the resource:** The rules for recording information about the source of the title proper have also gone through changes over time.
  - AACR2 rules require that the cataloger must always make a note that gives the source of the title proper for electronic

Example for e-book:
336	text $2 rdacontent
337	computer $2 rdamedia
338	online resource $2 rdacarrier

resources. It is entered in the MARC 500 field as a general note. They also require an "Item described" note: "For remote access resources, always give the date on which the resource was viewed for description."

- ○ The provider-neutral record guidelines suggest making the Source of title proper note except when a "Description based on print/other format version record (DBO) note is present." The Source of title proper note is entered in MARC field 500, while the Description based on note should be entered in the MARC 588 field.
- ○ RDA requires what is now called the Title Source note when the title is not taken from "the title page, title sheet, or title card (or image thereof) of a resource consisting of multiple pages, leaves, sheets, or cards (or images thereof)." The instructions here are accompanied by the same requirement that was present in AACR2 that one should also make a "note recording the date the resource was viewed." The notes are entered in the 500 field and the 588 field, respectively.

- **Variations in title:** It is not at all unusual for e-books to have a number of different titles on different resources.
  - ○ AACR2 rule 9.7.B4: "Make notes on titles borne by the item other than the title proper." The notes are generally entered in the 246 field with coding or text to provide an explanation of where on the piece they appear.
  - ○ PCC provider-neutral guidelines: These require only that the notes from the source record be retained but allow for notes on title variants in different providers' versions "if deemed important." It may be preceded by the text: "Available from some providers with title:" and also entered in field 246 (Culbertson, Mandelstam, and Prager, 2011: 6).
  - ○ RDA rules: There is no rule on adding variant titles that is specific to e-books. The general rules for cataloging all types of material apply equally to electronic resources. The Library of Congress has also included a policy statement continuing its policies for entering permutations of titles. They are also entered in field 246.

- **Summary note:** When rules were first formulated for cataloging electronic material, a Summary note was required. As the number of electronic resources has increased, however, the requirement has relaxed.
  - ○ AACR2 rule 9.7.B17 instructs catalogers of electronic resources to "Give a brief objective summary of the purpose and content of an item unless another part of the description provides enough information," resulting in a good many 520 fields being added to records.
  - ○ PCC provider-neutral guidelines make no mention of summaries. However, a related document, the *MARC Record Guide for Monograph Aggregator Vendors*, Second Edition

(Culbertson et al., 2009), encourages but does not require vendors to add summaries to records. Use the 520 field.

- RDA rules: There is no specific requirement for adding a summary for an electronic resource, only a general rule to add one "if it is considered to be important for identification or selection (e.g., for audiovisual resources or for resources designed for use by persons with disabilities) and sufficient information is not provided in another part of the description." Use the 520 field.

- **Other Formats/Additional Physical Form Entry:** Most e-books that are available today are also issued in print. There are differences in the way information about the alternative format is communicated to users in the three sets of rules:

- AACR2 rule 9.7B16 requires a note that records the details of other formats in which the resource is available. The note is entered in the MARC 530 field.

- PCC provider-neutral guidelines discourage the use of the Other Formats note in the 530 field but recommend that the cataloger "prefer subfield $i in the 776 field" (Culbertson, Mandelstam, and Prager, 2011: 8) and require it "if the description is based on the record for another format" (Culbertson, Mandelstam, and Prager, 2011: 10).

- RDA addresses this under rule 27.1.1.3, Referencing Related Manifestations, which includes examples of notes that are applicable to electronic resources. It is accompanied by a Library of Congress Policy Statement to the effect that except for records created using the single-record approach and those created using the provider-neutral record guidelines, catalogers should use the 775 field if the physical format of the original and the reproduction are the same and the 776 field if they are different.

Subject Cataloging

Because subject headings are not addressed in either AACR2 or RDA, it's not necessary to worry about changes between cataloging codes. In general there are no differences between the headings that you would assign to an e-book and those you would assign to a work in any other format.

It is not unusual, however, in order to enable retrieval of e-books through the library's catalog to add form/genre terms to the record. The term "Electronic books," although not authorized as a form/genre term either in *Library of Congress Subject Headings* (LCSH) or National Library of Medicine's *Medical Subject Headings* (MeSH), has been used frequently by libraries as a heading from an unspecified source.

Example:
655 4   Electronic books.

Added Entries

Make added entries according to the general rules in the code being used. In the case of a provider-neutral record, do not make added entries for bodies that are not responsible for all manifestations of the work.

Electronic Location and Access

The URL for an e-book is entered in the MARC 856 field in subfield **u**. The field indicators allow for the coding of the access method and the relationship "between the electronic resource at the location identified in field 856 and the item described in the record as a whole" (MARC 21: 856 field).

The 856 field is defined for the MARC holdings record as well as for the bibliographic record. For libraries using the MARC holdings record, it is useful to record the URLs in it, allowing the bibliographic record to serve for all versions.

Considerations for Batch Loading

Library systems vary in the way they import records. Some allow only record-by-record import. For those that do have a mechanism for batch loading records, the load mechanisms are specific to the system. There are some commonalities, however.

A duplicate detection and resolution mechanism is provided in most cases. As mentioned earlier, ensuring that your library system's matching algorithms work well with the numbers and codes in the records is essential. The matching algorithms may be used both in the process of loading records and in the process of deleting them. If the vendor changes the contents of an e-book collection every month, for example, and sends a new, up-to-date record set every month, the previous month's file can be used to identify the records for that load and mark them for deletion before adding the records for the current month. Alternatively, the vendor can send two lists, one of records to be deleted and the other of records to be added.

Batch loaders will generally flag records that have errors such as these: the MARC LDR is not formatted properly; the 001, 008, or 245 fields are duplicated; or if any of the fixed-length fields are not the proper length. They may also alert you to errors in the formatting of other fields, including subfields that are not defined for the field, unallowed duplication of fields or subfields, and errors in the 856 field, either in coding or in URL validation. They can also identify inconsistent or wrong character encoding and flag those errors. Check with your systems librarian or your vendor to find out what errors your loader will identify and whether it will produce a file of records to be reviewed or if it will simply discard the offending record.

It is a good idea to run a test batch for any new record sets to see what problems are inherent in them and how prevalent they are. This will give you an opportunity to make batch changes before loading the full set, which will save time and give better results. If you have access to a loading script that can identify conditional errors, it will give you even more options for cleaning up the cataloging without resorting to manual record-by-record editing.

Providing Added Value

Web users have come to expect far more from bibliographic records than they did before the advent of Amazon.com, LibraryThing, and Facebook. Despite having been warned, "Never judge a book by its cover," many still want to see a graphical representation of the book, preferably a colorful jacket. They also want access to the table of contents, previews, representative text, reviews, and links to information about the author. Whether you decide to include your e-books in your library catalog or to use a list on your website, you can include many of these services in your display.

There are several ways to acquire the data. Google, LibraryThing, Bowker, MARCIVE, OCLC, YBP, and a number of other companies offer services to enhance your records with such data. Some records are provided on an as-needed basis through application program interfaces (APIs), which are often free; others add data to the MARC record. These may require more investment but provide the benefit of becoming a permanent cataloging asset.

TechEssence.info (http://techessence.info/apis/) provides a list of library-related APIs that will allow you to enhance your catalog display in a remarkable number of ways, not only with cover graphics but also with lists of other editions and translations, author information, classification numbers, and more.

Conclusion

Catalogers and cataloging managers have always had to struggle with choosing the most cost-effective way to provide good access to library resources. They have also had to evaluate today's costs against tomorrow's benefits. Whatever decisions you make will be affected heavily by financial considerations, including those related to how to meet the financial challenges of the inevitable changes in technology, data formats, and cataloging rules. This chapter provides information on many of the issues you will face in cataloging e-books. A great deal more information is available on the web, in journal articles, and from your colleagues who have already learned from their successes and failures. For many years, librarians have put off making decisions about electronic resources, because the rate of change in that area was too great. Librarians know now that the rate of change is not about to slow down. Our patrons want and need e-books, and we can make them available only by using the tools that are here today, with an eye toward how we will make upgrades with the tools that we will have tomorrow.

References

Culbertson, Becky, Kate Harcourt, Yael Mandelstam, and George Prager. 2009. *MARC Record Guide for Monograph Aggregator Vendors*. Washington, DC: Program for Cooperative Cataloging. http://www.loc.gov/catdir/pcc/sca/FinalVendorGuide.pdf.

Culbertson, Becky, Yael Mandelstam, and George Prager. 2011. *Provider-Neutral E-Monograph MARC Record Guide*. Washington, DC: Program for Cooperative Cataloging. http://www.loc.gov/catdir/pcc/bibco/PN_Guide_20110915.pdf.

IFLA (International Federation of Library Associations) Study Group on the Functional Requirements for Bibliographic Records, and IFLA Section on Cataloguing Standing Committee. 1998. *Functional Requirements for Bibliographic Records*. Downloadable from the IFLA website. http://www.ifla.org/publications/functional-requirements-for-bibliographic-records.

International ISBN Agency. 2011. "International ISBN Agency FAQs." London: International ISBN Agency. http://www.isbn-international.org/faqs.

Joint Steering Committee for Development of RDA. 2011. *RDA: Resource Description & Access*. Chicago: American Library Association. http://access.rdatoolkit.org.

Joint Steering Committee for Revision of AACR, ed. 2005. *Anglo-American Cataloguing Rules*. 2nd, 2002 revision with 2005 update. Chicago: American Library Association. http://desktop.loc.gov/DocView/ESPAACR2/1.

Kelley, Michael. 2011. "Colorado Publishers and Libraries Collaborate on eBook Lending Model." *Library Journal* (March 17). http://www.libraryjournal.com/lj/home/889765-264/colorado_publishers_and_libraries_collaborate.html.csp.

Library of Congress. 2011. *MARC21 Format for Bibliographic Data*. Network Development and Library Standards Office. Update no. 1 (Oct. 2001) through Update No. 13 (Sept. 2011). Washington, DC: Library of Congress. http://www.loc.gov/marc/bibliographic/ecbdhome.html.

Martin, Kristin E., and Kavita Mundle. 2010. "Notes on Operations: Cataloging E-Books and Vendor Records: A Case Study at the University of Illinois at Chicago." *Library Resources and Technical Services* 54, no. 4 (October): 227–237.

OCLC. 2011. *Bibliographic Formats and Standards*. 4th ed. Dublin, OH: OCLC http://www.oclc.org/bibformats/default.htm.

OITP Task Force on E-Books (American Library Association Office for Information Technology Task Force on E-Books). 2011. "Frequently Asked E-Book Questions from Public Librarians." American Library Association. http://www.ala.org/offices/sites/ala.org.offices/files/content/oitp/e-book_faq.pdf.

Reese, Terry. 2009. "MarcEdit: Editing MARC Records Using the MarcEdit MarcEditor." *YouTube*. http://www.youtube.com/watch?v=kNMExHdki9k.

———. 2011. "About Me." *Terry's Worklog* (blog), October 4. http://people.oregonstate.edu/~reeset/blog/.

Sanchez, Elaine, and Paivi Rentz. 2011. *Transforming Collections, Transforming Technical Services: Finding Efficiencies in E-Content: Good Practices for Good Outcomes, Cataloging Efficiencies That Make a Difference: OCLC Forum at Texas State University, May 11, 2011*. SlideShare [database online]. http://www.slideshare.net/es02/transforming-collections-sanchez-oclc-may-6-2011-complete.

Assessment and Evaluation of E-Book Collections

Karen S. Grigg

Introduction

Librarians have used their expertise to collect both print and digital resources with the goal of serving their patrons and the institution (Richards and Eakin, 1997). For years, librarians employed the just-in-case philosophy in anticipation of what might be needed by students, faculty, clinicians, and researchers. It was thought that interlibrary loan requests should be few and that the materials should be available to patrons at the point of need. Assessment of purchasing decisions was relatively rare, as it was considered acceptable for research libraries to have collections that were infrequently used. Many libraries had the monograph budget to support this model. Highly specialized books were added to the collection in the event that they might eventually be used.

Many factors have led to sharp decreases in monies allocated to book collections. Tough economic times have led to reductions in library budgets. Academic and research libraries have taken large cuts in monograph budgets, as collection dollars are increasingly being diverted to accommodate the rising prices of journal subscriptions. Reported statistics from Association of Research Libraries (ARL) showed that, while the average cost for a monograph unit increased 78 percent from 1986 to 2006, the average price for a serial unit increased by 180 percent. Ultimately, the number of monographs purchased increased by a mere 1 percent during that time frame, while the number of serials purchased increased by 51 percent (Association of Research Libraries, 2006). Because the rising cost of serials is clearly impacting monograph budgets, it is no longer considered desirable to purchase books without employing some kind of assessment measures.

Although librarians have begun to implement systems for evaluating monograph collections using an evidence-based approach, many grapple with the challenges inherent in evaluating e-book purchases. Evidence-based librarianship "applies the best-available evidence, whether based upon either quantitative or qualitative research methods" and "encourages the pursuit of increasingly rigorous research strategies to support decisions affecting library practice" (Eldredge, 2000). Some librarians are attempting to develop standardized measures for analyzing the usage of electronic monographs and their relative value to the organization. In one such study, the University of Idaho Library used usage statistics and bibliographic data in order to determine whether or not e-books were being used and whether usage varies by subject area (Sprague and Hunter, 2008). A study done by Ugaz (2008) in a medical library found that usage of electronic monographs was much greater than that of their print counterparts, with a total of 12,123 uses and 278 circulations of e-books over a 14-month period. This chapter discusses some of the evidence-based methods that are and can be used to evaluate the relative success of collection decisions. Libraries are now using means such as balanced scorecard, circulation and usage statistics, survey measures, focus groups, and identification of strength areas of the institution as methods to ensure that book collections are vital and relevant. Additionally, the chapter discusses challenges collections librarians face using these methods and offers potential solutions.

Methods of Assessment

The following methods are described in this section:

- Usage data
- Overlap analysis
- Survey instruments
- Benchmarking
- Focus groups
- Balanced scorecard method

Usage Data

Librarians have often mined circulation statistics to determine the relative success of print monographs. These statistics can be used to determine which subject areas circulate most and what types of books tend to be used. Factors such as whether books that are heavily illustrated tend to be highly circulated, whether multivolume books circulate as well as single-volume books, and whether the books are more theoretical or practical can all be employed to drive future purchasing decisions. In addition, librarians can evaluate whether or not fiction tends to circulate more or less than nonfiction. E-books can be evaluated in the same manner. As with print monographs, the most obvious source of data would be usage data. Most publishers offer some kind of usage statistics that can be obtained from the vendor and examined. Usage statistics for each title can be analyzed and compared to one another, and lockouts can be examined. Often, when a concurrent user model is employed, librarians can start with one or two users and add additional users if frequent lockouts (meaning the number of simultaneous users exceeds the license agreement) occur.

While evaluation of usage data can be extremely helpful, there are challenges in comparing data from multiple sources. Definitions of a "search" and a "session" can vary from platform to platform. Librarians often believe that COUNTER-compliant statistics are the most valuable. COUNTER (Counting Online Usage of NeTworked Electronic Resources) is an international initiative that seeks to standardize the reporting of online usage statistics in a consistent manner. However, there are different methods of calculating COUNTER-compliant data, and these variations must be considered. There are six methods of calculating COUNTER statistics (COUNTER, 2006: Section 4):

BR1 = Book Report 1: Number of Successful Title Requests by Month and Title

BR2 = Book Report 2: Number of Successful Section Requests by Month and Title

BR3 = Turnaways by Month and Title

BR4 = Turnaways by Month and Service

BR5 = Total Searches and Sessions by Month and Title

BR6 = Total Searches and Sessions by Month and Service

If a vendor uses one of these methods in order to calculate searches and sessions, the statistics presented will differ from a vendor that uses another. Librarians should determine which COUNTER method is employed by each vendor and attempt to create a metric that can be used to compare apples to apples. For example, if one title uses **BR1** = Book Report 1: Number of Successful Title Requests by Month and Title and another uses **BR2** = Book Report 2: Number of Successful Section Requests by Month and Title, a librarian might try to calculate the average number of sections per a sample group of titles and divide the BR2 figures by that number to calculate what the average number of successful title requests might be for the title that uses BR2.

Another approach and one that might be most accurate is to identify which COUNTER method is used for each e-book package and choose to compare only titles with those other titles that use the same COUNTER code approach. User statistics can be imported into spreadsheets and sorted by subject area (or fiction versus nonfiction), and extrapolations can be made as to what subjects and formats are most often used.

Another factor that may skew usage statistics is the number of concurrent users allowed in each e-book title. If only one concurrent user is allowed for a specific e-book title and the book is highly used, the statistics may skew low, as users might be turned away. If turnaway numbers are available for books using the concurrent user model, it is important to review these numbers in order to make sense of the statistics presented. Finally, whenever one examines usage statistics, it is important to keep in mind that usage data does not indicate the usefulness of a title to the patron. An e-book may be chosen because it has been promoted heavily or because it is presented high in a list of search results. A user might access a title, yet not find it useful or relevant. When user statistics are examined, it is important to identify which titles and packages use a concurrent usage model and then take this into consideration, as titles with a low number of simultaneous users might tend to show less usage. If the vendor provides lockout statistics, these numbers might be added to the number of uses to provide a fuller picture, as a lockout can be considered an attempted use.

Overlap Analysis

Overlap analysis can be done with products such as the Serials Solutions 360 Core Overlap Analysis tool or the EBSCO A-to-Z list and is a method that can provide librarians with information about unique holdings as well as duplications. Overlap analysis can query, for each database in a library's collection, the number of titles in that database that are unique to that database and the number that are available elsewhere in the library's collection. Although this method is mainly employed with journal collections, some products can do this with e-book packages and compare titles by subject area, looking for both gaps and overlaps. Overlap analysis can identify titles that are duplicated and allow librarians to make cancellations, thus freeing budget dollars. Additionally, overlap analysis can identify subject areas that need enhancement. While this data can be useful in order to identify potential cancellations, there are limitations that must be considered. Unfortunately, some duplication cannot be avoided. If two versions of an e-book are included in an e-book package, neither title may be eligible for cancellation. Additionally, one version of an e-book might be preferable to another, and librarians need to evaluate both copies for such factors as ease of navigation, inclusions of graphs and illustrations, and potential negative financial consequences of cancellations that may be imposed by the vendor.

Survey Instruments

Libraries often employ user survey instruments to evaluate user impressions of library collections. These surveys can stand alone, or questions about e-books can be folded into larger, more general library surveys and query users as to how they feel about the increasing availability of e-books, what e-books they have used, and what the users perceive as gaps in the collection. Although surveys can be useful in terms of determining patrons' perceptions of e-books and what patrons need in library collections, results provided by these instruments must be used in conjunction with other assessment measures. Often, results can be skewed by the fact that only the most motivated users will take the time to fill out surveys. Patrons who answer surveys are often those who hold strong feelings about a topic, and results can be skewed to the extremes. Some librarians offer incentives, such as prizes, in order to entice a wider spectrum of patrons to complete surveys. Additionally, patrons who don't actually use e-book collections may still indicate positive impressions of library e-book collections, as most library users will tend to agree in theory that availability of e-books is a positive thing. Finally, if querying patrons for feedback on subject areas that might be desired for the collection, libraries are likely to find that users will naturally indicate their area of research or interest rather than a general assessment of what subject areas would be useful for the collection as a whole. Methods of enticing greater numbers of users to respond, as well as careful crafting of survey questions, can help mitigate these challenges.

These are some potential questions that could be used in a survey:

- Have you used e-books in the library's collection?
- If yes, how many have you used? (1–3, 4–6, 7–9, 10+)
- If yes, why did you choose to use this e-book? (I needed this title, and it was only available in electronic format; I was able to access this title without going to the physical library.)
- If a book is available in print and electronic format, which would you be most likely to use?
- Are you more likely to prefer an e-book for a fiction or non-fiction format?
- Does the e-book collection at this library satisfy your needs? If not, why not?

Benchmarking

One method of assessing the quality of a library's e-book collection is to compare library holdings to other libraries. In order to begin, it is important to identify one's peer institutions. Consider these factors when selecting peers:

- Size of library
- Similarity of subject areas covered
- Library's total e-book budget, if this can be determined (Some collection development librarians will share this information freely.)
- Library ranking (Is there a source that ranks libraries of this type? It is most helpful to select libraries that are similarly ranked.)

Once a handful of peer institutions have been identified, librarians can search the library's catalog and study the library's website to determine the scope and holdings of the library's e-book collection. Sometimes, this data is not easy to extract. If not, it may be helpful to find a collection development contact and ask about the library's e-book collections.

Focus Groups

While surveys provide quantitative data that can be used to provide evidence-based decision making, focus groups allow for qualitative querying. Gathering a diverse group of users and asking open-ended questions allows for creative brainstorming of ideas and tapping into free-flowing conversation that may bring forth ideas and concepts that could not be captured by a survey instrument. Focus groups can also look at the strengths and weaknesses of a collection as well as help evaluate

ONLINE SURVEY RESOURCES

Online surveys are easy to create and distribute. Here are a couple of useful sites that allow one to create survey instruments:

- SurveyMonkey: http://www.surveymonkey.com/
- Zoomerang: http://www.zoomerang.com/

publishers' platforms, navigability, and format. However, using focus groups as a sole method of seeking user feedback can be problematic. Focus groups work only with small groups, so ideas presented might be specific to the few individuals who participate. Additionally, a lack of anonymity may inhibit criticism that is important for the library to consider. Often, larger incentives, such as free lunch, may entice users to participate who actually have little to add to the discussion. Additionally, a skillful mediator must be used in order to keep participants on topic and to move the discussion along. Finally, certain user groups, such as faculty and researchers, may be hard to gather, as these users tend to be over-extended and disinclined to participate. Focus groups can provide useful feedback but should be employed with other methods of assessment. Mentch, Strauss, and Zsulya (2008) discuss the use of focus groups in a library setting in order to assess the efficacy of collection management.

Balanced Scorecard Method

The balanced scorecard method, first proposed by Robert Kaplan and David Norton in 1992, is a strategic approach and performance management system that can be employed to identify critical success factors and translate these into performance measures that can be tracked over time. Organizations can determine both financial and nonfinancial successful outcomes, identify means of measuring these outcomes, calculate and analyze these measures, and use results as a reporting tool. For example, a library that employs the balanced scorecard method might have a segment for collection success that uses circulation statistics as a successful outcome measure. One measure could be that "80 percent of the e-books purchased this calendar year will have at least 100 searches and sessions." At the end of the calendar year, results can be analyzed and presented. Improvements can be measured by setting a slightly more ambitious goal the following year, such as "85 percent of the monographs purchased this calendar year will have at least 150 searches and sessions." These are tools that can be used to present to administrators data-driven results that show the success of the collection management team. While this method can legitimize the work of collection managers, many question the overall effectiveness of employing this method. Certainly, using the balanced scorecard alone will not identify what kinds of e-books are more useful than others but merely will show whether or not e-books are being used. Additionally, results are only as good as the measures, and it can be challenging to identify realistic or even relevant measures of success.

Other Factors That Present Challenges in Making and Assessing Purchasing Decisions

Some of the many methods of assessing effectiveness of e-book purchasing decisions have been identified, along with potential challenges to using

---

ASSESSMENT RESOURCES

The following is a helpful guide for assessment and outcome measurement of library services and resources:

- Farnam Dudden, Rosalind. 2007. *Using Benchmarking, Needs Assessment, Quality Improvement, Outcome Measurement, and Library Standards: A How-To-Do-It Manual for Librarians with CD-ROM.* A Medical Library Association Guide. New York: Neal-Schuman.

The following site allows one to compare two or more e-book platforms in order to run a comparison:

- JISC Academic Database Assessment Tool. "Academic Database Assessment Tool: Compare eBook Platforms." JISC Collections. http://www.jisc-adat.com/adat/adat_ebooks.pl.

these methods. One challenge with evaluating e-book purchases is that applying criteria and principles used for evaluating print monographs are not always directly applicable to e-books. Because e-books are not physical objects that can be unavailable for extended periods of time, and because e-books are more convenient for users because of remote access, the least used e-book may still show more usage than some of the more used print books. While some business models allow for multiple users, others do not allow the e-book to be utilized if the title is "checked out" by someone else. It is important to understand the particulars of each package's business model in order to make sense of the usage statistics. If a library determines that two loans per year is considered acceptable use, how does one make sense of an e-book that shows 20 uses when compared to another title with hundreds of uses? Librarians must determine the minimum number of uses that are realistic to expect an e-book to incur, keeping in mind the differences that are used in calculating searches and sessions. If a median or mode number of uses can be identified overall, standard deviations can be identified and used to calculate the relative success of an individual title. Librarians can calculate the average number of times an e-book has been used and calculate, identify standard deviations, and then decide what is considered "acceptable." Books that fall within or less than two standard deviations of the mean can be identified as those with "unacceptable" levels of circulation. Other issues are important to consider as well:

- Lack of impact factors
- Issues with e-book readers
- Availability from multiple vendors

Lack of Impact Factors

Collection managers have been employing data-driven means of determining viability of journal titles for many years, as electronic journals were the first electronic resources available and heavily purchased in libraries. Librarians who wished to assess the relative efficacy of e-journal packages often used the journal impact factor as data to accompany usage statistics. A low-used title might be retained if it had a high impact factor and few titles were available in that subject area. Librarians who are accustomed to using impact factors to determine the importance of a journal title can be frustrated by the lack of information as the importance of a specific monograph title. Book reviews can be studied to provide a minimal level of feedback as to whether a title is authoritative or core. One method employed with both print and electronic subscriptions is that of the journal impact factor. Unfortunately, this means is not available for monographs, so librarians have to rely on reviews or core/recommended lists from professional associations in order to guess at the relative quality of a monograph. So when assessing an e-book collection for retention or value, it is important to consider whether that title is considered a core or major publication in the field (similar to a journal impact factor), as well as usage statistics.

Peer comparisons are often used to determine how a library's collection stacks up to that of its peer institutions. Tools like the WorldCat Collection Analysis Tool (http://www.oclc.org/collectionanalysis/) can identify gaps in subject areas and can identify specific book titles that might be relevant for the library. This tool compares the several peer institutions and identifies the number of unique titles in each LC subject heading. Although peer comparisons are possible when assessing print collections, this method is less than useful when comparing e-book collections. Libraries do not always add their holdings of e-books to OCLC, as e-books cannot be used for interlibrary loan, and thus librarians often assume that other institutions would not need or desire to see holdings for titles that cannot be borrowed. Because print titles are considered to be "owned," while e-book titles are considered to be "accessed," libraries tend not to list holdings for e-book collections such as ebrary, where titles can change over time.

Issues with E-Book Readers

Many libraries have begun to circulate e-book readers, such as Kindles and Nooks. These devices can prove problematic for librarians who wish to analyze circulation statistics. E-book readers can generally be a challenge for libraries, as these devices are generally intended for the individual reader rather than for institutions. Certainly, it is not difficult to examine the number of times an individual e-book reader has circulated. However, it is not readily apparent how many times a particular book title has been accessed on the e-book reader. To evaluate the use of e-book reader titles, other assessment measures, such as survey instruments or focus groups, can be used. Kindles are particularly troublesome in the library setting, as Amazon has determined that these devices cannot be circulated with preloaded electronic content; thus, these readers may soon disappear from libraries.

When using data to make purchasing decisions, the data must be considered in conjunction with other factors, such as these:

- Is the title part of a larger package? If so, what are the cancellation terms of this package?
- Is the e-book package part of a larger consortial deal?
- Was the title purchased outright with one-time dollars and thus not eligible for cancellation?
- Is the title in a narrow or specialized subject area? (Note: this might not be as important in a research library setting, where patrons might specialize in narrow topics.)
- Does the library retain perpetual access?
- Will there be any financial penalty for cancellation?

These factors must be weighed and examined before making any cancellations.

Availability from Multiple Vendors

Often, an e-book may be available from more than one vendor. In cases of title duplication, librarians may decide that one copy will suffice. In order to choose the best vendor, when the book is available on more than one platform, consider these factors:

- Is there a significant price difference? If so, the cheaper e-book might be more desirable.

- Which platform has better navigability? Evaluation by library staff and patrons might help determine this.

- Does one platform have higher quality graphics?

- Does one vendor impose cancellation penalties? If the library's budget is decreased, will it be possible to cancel the subscription without paying a fee?

- Is the title part of a larger package? If so, does the library already subscribe to the package? If not, are the other titles of interest?

- What is the business model? Does the library prefer one-time purchases, which require repurchase of newer editions, or are subscriptions more desirable?

It's important to evaluate a variety of factors other than usage in order to determine which title is a better candidate for cancellation or retention.

Future Trends

Future trends in the e-book horizon will create challenges for librarians who choose to use evidence-based methods for assessment. As discussed in Chapter 2, publishers are still grappling with business models for selling and leasing e-books and will continue to change business terms. As these models evolve, license terms may prove to make cancellations more difficult. The careful selection techniques discussed in Chapter 5 will help libraries minimize the purchase of scarcely used titles. As librarians develop more robust and standardized methods for evaluating use, this information must be employed in order to drive future purchasing decisions. Statistics can be further explored to reveal subject areas that garner high e-book use and format types that are most desirable. It is becoming increasingly common to gather a variety of statistics, but if these statistics are not used to drive future decision making, they will be of little use to the institution.

Data-driven collection analysis may show a sharp increase in e-book usage and a decline in print book usage. When examining this data, librarians should determine how much a print monograph collection is valued by the institution. As detailed in Chapter 7, researchers, faculty, and students in certain subject areas such as medicine or science might show a strong preference for e-books, and thus libraries that specialize in these subject areas might decide to sharply decrease budget dollars allotted for print materials and increase allotments for e-books. In other subject areas, selections may be scant and patrons in these fields of study may not be prepared to make the transition. Data is important in order to drive decision making, but intrinsic values of the institution are also important considerations. Over time, the numbers of available titles will most likely increase, and librarians will need to further grapple with defining the relative importance of having physical book titles on the shelves.

Additionally, the MP3-influenced younger generation has driven publishers to make it possible to increasingly download specific book chapters rather than having to purchase entire textbooks. This focus on downloading partial content is already a growing trend and will most likely become even more prevalent. Will this trend leave librarians and libraries out of the book selection process? How will libraries purchase or lease portions of books? It's possible that user licenses will evolve to exclude institutions and favor the individual purchaser.

Conclusion

The decline in library collection budgets will make evaluation and assessment of purchasing decisions increasingly important. Librarians who employ techniques for evaluation of print monographs or electronic journals will find that these methods must be tweaked in order to gather useful data for e-book purchasing evaluation. By utilizing a variety of techniques, such as evaluation of usage statistics, overlap analysis, survey instruments, focus groups, and methods borrowed from the business literature such as the balanced scorecard, librarians can overcome the challenges inherent in using only one data source. This data, combined with knowledge of information about e-books such as licensing terms, business models, cost data, and subject and format analysis, can help librarians make better future purchasing decisions that will enhance collections and best serve patrons.

The ultimate goals of assessment of e-book purchases should be to purchase more relevant titles and to drive greater usage of the titles that the library adds to the collection. Assessment should be combined with promotion of the existing e-book collections, as promotion will help increase awareness and enthusiasm and ultimately lead to higher use. Patrons should have the ability to link to desired e-book content directly from the library catalog so that they do not have to perform another search or navigate through a lengthy table of contents. Librarians should ensure that access to e-book titles is consistent and reliable for mobile devices, such as smartphones. E-book collections should be promoted through newsletters, blog entries, and website real estate. Catalog layers and enhancements, such as book cover display, ability to view table of contents, and electronic bookshelves can enhance the possibility for serendipitous discovery, which is a challenge with electronic resources. Finally, reference and instruction librarians should be aware of the breadth and depth of the library's e-book collections and promote these offerings to patrons whenever possible.

Proper assessment of e-book collections goes beyond traditional print selection strategies of examining the need for titles in specific subject areas and the reputations of authors and publishers. It also goes beyond analyzing usage statistics to see, in retrospect, if the titles were appropriate and well used. Assessment of e-book collections needs to also take into consideration access and format issues and the quality of publishers' and aggregators' platforms. Leasing versus ownership of e-resources will also affect how a collection is assessed, as will licensing issues involving preservation, copyright, and interlibrary lending. This chapter, and the book as a whole, points out the complexities and best practice solutions for building and managing e-book collections.

References

Association of Research Libraries. 2006. "ARL Statistics 2005–2006: Monograph and Serial Expenditures in ARL Libraries, 1986–2006." Association of Research Libraries. Accessed October 28, 2011. http://www.arl.org/bm~doc/monser06.pdf.

COUNTER. 2006. "The COUNTER Code of Practice. Books and Reference Works: Release 1." The COUNTER Project. http://www.projectcounter.org/cop_books_ref.pdf.

Eldredge, James. 2000. "Evidence-Based Librarianship: An Overview." *Bulletin of the Medical Library Association* 88, no. 4: 289–302.

Kaplan, Robert, and David P. Norton. 1992. "The Balanced Scorecard—Measures That Drive Performance." *Harvard Business Review* 70, no. 1: 71–79.

Mentch, Fran, Barbara Strauss, and Carol Zsulya. 2008. "The Importance of 'Focusness': Focus Groups as a Means of Collection Management Assessment." *Collection Management* 33, no. 1: 115–128.

Richards, Daniel T., and Dottie Eakin. 1997. *Collection Development and Assessment in Health Sciences Libraries*. Lanham, MD: Medical Library Association and Scarecrow Press.

Sprague, Nancy, and Ben Hunter. 2008. "Assessing E-Books: Taking a Closer Look at E-Book Statistics." *Library Collections, Acquisitions, and Technical Services* 32, no. 3–4:150–157.

Ugaz, A.G. 2008. "Assessing Print and Electronic Use of Reference/Core Medical Textbooks." *Journal of the Medical Library Association* 96, no. 2: 145–147.

E-Books in Practice

E-Books in a High School Library— Cushing Academy

Tom Corbett

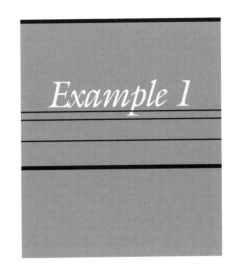

Example 1

Introduction

Cushing Academy, an independent New England boarding school, made headlines in the fall of 2009 by announcing that it was donating its 20,000 paper-based book collection to area libraries and going entirely "bookless." A front-page article in the *Boston Globe*, with a picture of our Academy's headmaster, Dr. James Tracy, standing amid broken down bookshelves and scratching his head, conveyed an impression of trepidation and doubt (Abel, 2009). In reality, the decision was made both confidently and strategically as part of our long-range plan to build a "21st Century Leadership" curriculum.

Of course, the library was awash in books after the transformation; they were just electronic books ("e-books") rather than paper-based books ("p-books"). In fact, the Academy's library collection provides real-time access to more than one million copyrighted monographs, made immediately available through its two primary e-book vendors, Amazon and Ebook Library (EBL). However, the most controversial aspect of our transformation was not the decision to add e-books but rather *to remove a majority of our p-books*. The rationale behind that decision was that the library staff would be able to focus its efforts on this new e-book medium without dividing its time and resources on supporting an extensive p-book collection. Not only did this free up significant floor space to be used for other library and institutional purposes, but it also allowed the staff to abandon certain traditional tasks in order to spend more time and resources developing new and expanded library services (Corbett, 2011). This E-Books in Practice example explores what has worked well and not as well as a result of this paradigm shift from p-books to e-books in a secondary school library.

The Secondary School Library's Two Main Roles: Support for Research and Reading

To properly evaluate (and implement) the use of e-books in a secondary school setting, it is important to distinguish two services this type of library provides: namely, *research* and *reading*. *Teaching* is another essential school library service, growing in importance because of the increased need for information literacy in the twenty-first-century education paradigm, but not directly related to the use of e-books.

E-Books Serving the Library's Research Role

In its research role, the secondary school library is not intended to be a permanent storehouse of society's knowledge but rather a resource for students and teachers to explore topics beyond those found in the classroom textbooks or teacher lectures. Of course, the growth of the Internet has significantly challenged this role and arguably made a relatively small nonfiction monograph collection even smaller and less valuable. It is still an open question, even at our Academy, as to whether a nonfiction monograph collection—whether composed of p-books, e-books, or a combination of the two—adds enough value for us to justify its costs.

One important advantage that nonfiction e-books have over their paper-based counterparts is that content can be fully indexed and integrated into the library's search environment. However, this requires a partnership with an e-book vendor that provides indexed access to e-books as well as a partnership with a federated search vendor that can essentially combine this index with the indexes of other library database resources. Out of the handful of vendors that can provide these services, Cushing Academy has contracted with two: EBL and Deep Web Technologies. Both business partnerships are essential to fully exploiting the power of e-books in service to the library's research role.

EBL (http://www.eblib.com/) provides us with fully indexed access to nearly 200,000 e-books, largely from academic presses and mostly nonfiction. This service takes full advantage of the e-book paradigm by allowing immediate access to titles not necessarily owned by the library. Rather than having to purchase the content up front, the library is charged only *after* students and teachers discover and utilize e-book content as part of the research process. As a result, our users have immediate access to a much larger set of monographic content than before. This important patron-driven acquisitions (PDA) process—or perhaps better described as a real-time *research*-driven acquisitions process—is possible only within a digital environment. Moreover, within this paradigm smaller libraries (such as secondary school libraries) can limit their costs based on lower usage requirements and not by reducing the number of monographs they provide access to. The cost of library services becomes more a function of usage rather than collection size.

This integration of nonfiction e-book content is made even more effective through the use of a federated search service. At Cushing, we subscribe to Explorit, a federated search service created by Deep Web Technologies (http://www.deepwebtech.com/), but other integration services, such as Summons from ProQuest, are also available. These services place e-book content on an equal footing with database content by combining the search results into one "Google-like" experience for our users (and, like any good search engine, re-ranking the results based on relevancy). As a result, students and teachers discover content from non-fiction monographs alongside journals, online encyclopedias, and other digital library resources.

The e-book medium also allows monographic content to be more easily embedded in the classroom's digital space, or portal. Monographs identified by library staff and teachers as being particularly helpful at augmenting class materials can be highlighted and made available 24/7 from within the class page and/or on a library page dedicated to that course (a LibGuide, for example). Potentially, chapters or even pages from the monograph can be posted and shared while still protecting copyright. While some of this functionality is dependent on the quality of the e-book hosting platform itself, the process is made easier by using a sophisticated software platform on the library's end. At Cushing Academy, we have built our site using Drupal, an open source content management system (CMS). This highly adaptable platform has allowed us to create dynamic pages dedicated to particular courses and embeddable within the learning management system (LMS) used throughout the school. The end result essentially brings the library's reserve shelf and related services into each classroom, available 24/7 and, depending on the vendor platform, available for concurrent usage.

However, despite these initiatives, the use of e-books in support of our library's research role has not fully lived up to expectations. Usage has been only slightly higher than in recent years with our p-book collection. Perhaps monographs have been replaced by Internet resources and online databases as a preferred teacher's resource; or perhaps our selection of e-book titles, as large as it is, is still too highly academic for secondary school students; or perhaps we just have not given our efforts enough time to take root and be successful.

E-Books Serving the Library's Reading Role

A second and equally important role for a secondary school is to encourage "deep," immersive reading, often not directly tied to the classroom curriculum. This is a role one can argue still fits well with p-books. In fact, in our library we still actively collect picture p-books for our small children's library, serving the young children of faculty and visitors. While tablet devices, such as the Apple iPad or the many Android-based options, can offer a new immersive "reading" experience for young readers, we feel this technology best supplements rather than replaces printed picture books. However, text-based books for older readers are another story. Here we feel e-readers provide a quality reading experience even exceeding that of the printed book. While p-books still provide a few unique advantages, it is debatable whether these advantages warrant the resources needed to adequately provide for them in a secondary school environment. In our view, they do not; the opportunity costs are simply too high.

E-books support the library's reading role by allowing for greater choice, easier integration with social media, and improved portability. By allowing for "just-in-time" (JiT) and patron-driven acquisition (PDA) business models, the e-book environment can greatly expand choice and allow students to access a much larger universe of popular reading materials than typically found in a small, locally stored p-book collection. At Cushing Academy, we encourage our students to explore the entire Amazon e-book collection, using the social media services found through that platform to discover new authors and genres. We also direct students to EBSCO's Novelist Plus and Gale's Books and Authors for further exploration, with the immediate availability of the books determined by their availability as Kindle e-books rather than by whether or not they have previously been purchased and are "in our collection." Once a title is requested by our users, its acquisition is still mediated and processed by library staff, albeit very quickly. In this way our Kindle reading program, unlike EBL for academic nonfiction, is more of a "patron-driven *demand*" rather than a "patron-driven *acquisition*" process. Titles discovered by our students and faculty are purchased upon request and transferred to either the next available Kindle at the circulation desk or directly to one already checked out. Students are told to keep the Kindle for as long as they continue reading, with new titles purchased and delivered wirelessly to them upon request. In this way, students have immediate access to a much larger collection of reading materials than ever before.

Of course, the value of electronic text, especially for extended reading, is directly correlated with the quality of the device it is displayed on. In this regard, paper sets a very high standard. This is why we primarily deliver our reading service through nearly 100 e-ink–based Kindles rather than through laptops or even tablet devices. As many have discovered, given the success of the Kindle and Nook, the quality of the e-ink reading experience rivals that of the paper-based book, but with the added transformative benefits of digitization. For an institution able to dedicate its resources to this technology and ensure that the availability of these devices is not a barrier to access, the advantages are significant. Rows of books disappear, freeing up valuable floor space; users gain nearly immediate access to over one million titles, not just a few thousand; staff spends more time talking about books rather than shelving them; and students can walk out of the library carrying an entire fantasy series in one hand rather than leaving frustrated that the first book is missing or checked out. All of this leads to the most important measurement of success: significantly more long-form reading.

Conclusion

In fact, it is in the service of the library's reading role that Cushing Academy's leap into this future has been most successful. Perhaps initially because of the uniqueness of the e-readers, long-form popular reading increased dramatically during the first year of the program. Fortunately, this increase has not slowed, partly because of the quality of the e-reading experience itself. Along with the consistent quality of the font tailored to the reader's own preferences, students tell us they also like the immediacy of the online dictionary and, especially among our ESL students, the voice-to-text feature. Students often remark that they are not only reading more, but more quickly on the Kindle e-readers. We also think greatly expanded choice and the immediate availability of titles made possible by a PDA and JiT approach to delivering digital reading content have further fueled this success. Even with the same book budget as before, our library simply has better tools in a digital environment to discover and meet—and even create—demand.

However, as noted earlier, the library cannot point to the same success servicing its research role through e-books. Despite a more sophisticated approach to interjecting this content into the library's discovery tools, usage has not grown considerably. Students still regularly click past this content just as they walked past rows of nonfiction books earlier. However, the use of subscription content *of all types* has remained mostly stagnant over the past few years. Hopefully this usage will improve as we continue to promote its use and simplify initial access to this content by "embedding" library staff within the classroom, improving the federated search process, and encouraging faculty to set higher standards for student research.

Our experience at Cushing Academy has shown that e-books can be part of a resurgence of library services within secondary schools as long as we continue working with publishers and distributors to develop sustainable services that take full advantage of the unique qualities of digital content delivery.

ACTIONS TO IMPROVE LIBRARY SERVICES BY PRIORITIZING DIGITAL CONTENT

- Establish PDA and JiT services to allow students to explore the larger universe of reading rather than focusing on a limited local collection.
- Encourage distraction-free, immersive reading by utilizing e-ink-based devices.
- Focus on a federated search that tightly integrates e-books with other subscription content rather than defaulting to a search based on a limited local collection.
- Work directly with faculty to match the library's digital content to the curriculum, integrating it into course portals, available 24/7.
- Provide online support to help students who are using the library remotely.
- Work with faculty to raise citation standards and promote ethical research.

References

Abel, David. 2009. "Welcome to the Library. Say Goodbye to the Books." *Boston Globe*, September 4. http://www.boston.com/news/local/massachusetts/articles/2009/09/04/a_library_without_the_books/.

Corbett, Thomas B. 2011 "The Changing Role of the School Library's Physical Space." *School Library Monthly* 27, no 7: 5. http://www.schoollibrarymonthly.com/articles/Corbett2011-v27n7p5.html.

Marketing E-Books in a Public Library—Half Hollow Hills Community Library

Ellen Druda

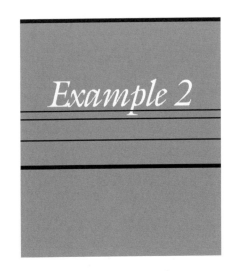

Example 2

E-Books and the Public Library— Read, Pray, Love

Working as an Internet Services Librarian at the Half Hollow Hills Community Library in suburban Dix Hills, New York, I've had many opportunities to introduce our patrons to computer and web services. When e-book service began in our library, we were delighted that there was some newfound excitement in reading in this format. We want our library patrons to read, we want them to love what they've discovered, and we want them to be able to share their thoughts about what they've read. But one thing we can always bank on is whenever we introduce any element of technology, no matter how well prepared and practiced we are, it always calls for a bit of luck for things to function the way we want, especially if we're dealing with an audience of patrons who are new to electronic resources. No doubt that is when the Internet slows down, and your computer decides to freeze. But, when things do go right, we love the results and can see our patrons loving it too.

E-Book Demand Is Growing

E-books were available for patron downloading beginning in 2008, and less than 100 circulated. The statistics almost doubled the next year, and by 2010 e-book circulation was approaching 1,200. The curve continues to rise dramatically, and by the end of 2011, 10,451 e-books were downloaded. The demand has impacted budgeting for print books (p-books), and that story is probably similar in most public libraries that offer e-books. With new devices and tablets being offered that will work with our e-book lending service (OverDrive), new publishers testing the e-book waters, and Amazon's decision to allow Kindle owners to participate in the library program, there is no reason to think e-books won't remain popular for quite some time. Our library patrons check them out faster than we can add to the collection.

Reader Types in a Public Library

The library's reading public can be sorted into three types: the patrons who are comfortable reading in nontraditional formats, such as on an e-book reader, computer, or other mobile devices; the patrons who still check out our p-books and attend book discussion groups; and those who are somewhere in between. Despite the dramatic and continual rise in e-book circulation, most of our readers fall into the third group. Many are curious about the new technology and would be willing to try it but are still using p-books for various reasons. One reason so many of our patrons still prefer p-books is the familiar feel. Almost all of us have grown up with books in the traditional print format, and it resonates with memories of what "reading" is. P-books were ours as children and through most of our adult life, and we've handled them and learned to read using them. For some, adjusting to reading on a screen for pleasure is a difficult one. It looks and feels different. Another reason is accessibility— there are many more p-books available for checkout at any one time. This may change in the future.

Book Discussion Groups—P but Not E

Most of our book group discussion members are traditional p-book users. When I brought e-book devices to several meetings, I was hoping for a positive reaction, but many questioned the need or practicality of the devices and/or had difficulty using them and navigating around the text. Despite what our e-book circ stats told us, a segment of our patrons still enjoyed reading and sharing with traditional print media.

Encouraging the Use of E-Books

First and foremost, we need the staff to be comfortable with the technology of e-books. Because not all staff members own their own e-book readers, the library purchased a Sony Reader, a Nook, a Kobo, and an iPad, along with a laptop computer for them to work with. All librarians have been trained on using the devices, but we found that while training is important, it's best to have the devices handy and available near the librarians' desks for them to practice with and also assist patrons. If a librarian is uncomfortable with the technology, that feeling will transfer to the patrons. The public service desk is a busy place, and it's not always easy to take the time to demonstrate e-books, but if they are left out in a secure place at least it should remind everyone that e-books are available. This was accomplished by creating a little "petting zoo" of e-book readers on a small table a few feet away from the reference desk. It's also located next to our Internet computers, so it is in a high-traffic area. An "Electronic Petting Zoo" sign in a bright neon font draws attention, and attached to the table is a laptop, color Nook, iPad, and Kobo reader, and a Kindle will be joining the zoo soon. The devices are secured using a removable cable lock and left in a password-protected mode, so a librarian needs to intervene if a patron wants more than a casual look. That gives us a chance to interact with our users who might be interested in e-book reading but haven't had the chance to try it out for themselves. The area has served as a passive reminder about the technology and a place for ad hoc demonstrations.

The petting zoo has also reinforced the idea of the library as technology trainer for the public. We offer one-to-one computer training sessions for our patrons, handled by screened and trained student and senior volunteers. These volunteers are also trained in downloading e-books and are available some evenings and weekends, usually more convenient for our patrons who may need help.

Marketing E-Books

Marketing the service is vital. Our library used the traditional methods: flyers, posters, bookmarks, links on our website, Facebook page, and Twitter feed. We use Facebook and Twitter as most libraries do—as a way to communicate timely information and promote our services in general—but they can be the most effective tool to market our digital services, because we know our fans and followers are already online. Our rule: one Facebook post and tweet a day, minimum. Whenever we are working on a specific campaign, our social networking is always a part.

We also placed a large banner outside the building and had every staff member wearing a button that said "Ask Me About eBooks." Distributed along with the button was a very short printed script so that all staff (including pages) would have an answer prepared if they were asked. Here's an example of the script:

1. E-books are downloadable books that you can read with an e-reader such as Barnes & Noble's Nook, the Sony Reader, etc.

2. There are thousands of books to choose from. You can find them by clicking on the "Live-brary" link from our website (http://www.hhhlibrary.org/).

3. Books will automatically disappear after 7 or 14 days. No fines or overdues. If a title is out, you can reserve it just like a book, and you will be notified by e-mail when it is available.

4. See a librarian for a demonstration on downloading e-books from Live-brary.

5. For questions contact Ellen Druda ext. . . .

We also had a visit from the OverDrive Digital Bookmobile during the summer. The Digital Bookmobile is actually a large trailer truck sponsored and sent by OverDrive to select libraries. It is staffed with OverDrive experts and is full of equipment for patrons to test out downloading media. The trailer stayed in the parking lot for two days (one day at each library building) and was open to the public. Those who entered were given a "guided tour" on downloading with the various e-readers, video, and MP3 players.

Our campaigns are the result of regular strategy meetings that include permanent members of the marketing committee and a rotating group of "experts." The permanent committee members include a representative from the adult reference department, the library director and/or assistant director, the head of youth services, the head of teen services, our programs and publicity department head, and a representative from our branch. Depending on what we are promoting, the committee will invite the library's "expert" in the field to help form and participate in the campaign. For example, promoting a free music downloading service will include the librarians in charge of ordering music; the campaign to increase database usage will include the librarian in charge of selecting databases. The e-book campaign included the head of our adult services department, who does most of the fiction book selection, and the Internet services librarian, who also handles technology training. We found that when we coordinated our ideas, art, and words throughout the departments and buildings, we were most effective in getting that message out to our patrons. All the signs, buttons, displays, bookmarks, posters, and so forth said the same thing.

Probably the most effective marketing was done by sheer luck through forces outside the library, such as Amazon and Barnes & Noble's own marketing of their e-book readers, especially during the Christmas shopping season. Suddenly a large group of patrons became aware that e-books and e-readers even existed and, better yet, wanted to buy them for gifts. With patron awareness rising, we also booked a visit from a representative of Barnes & Noble, who did an evening program on downloading to the Nook. That was popular for that third group of patrons who were interested in e-books but not totally comfortable with the technology. It brought in those who were thinking about purchasing a Nook, who had recently received one as a gift, or who were just generally curious. It's a program we will be repeating on our own.

E-Books into the Book Discussion Program

Another marketing strategy was starting our first e-book discussion program. We chose *iDrakula*, by Becca Black. This was an unusual book because it was available in multiple formats: a printed graphic novel, a downloadable e-book, and an iPhone app. To make it even more appealing, the author made an appearance via Skype and chatted with our audience. The program attracted mostly teens, and we discovered that all formats were utilized—some had read the p-book, some had downloaded it to their computers, and some brought it with them on their mobile devices.

Book Discussion Summit

Our next goal is to integrate all our readers into the same book discussion groups. Our hope is to have the p-book readers and the e-book readers enjoying the same content and sharing ideas. We have many book discussion groups in our community; some we sponsor, but most are run by individuals outside of the library. We have a librarian specifically devoted to helping the leaders of these groups get the books they want for all their members in addition to providing readers advisory. The leaders were contacted by e-mail, telephone, and regular mail and invited to a Book Discussion Summit, a chance for them to exchange ideas about books and running book clubs. We also invited a local television book reviewer to talk about his favorite books. Including another demonstration of downloading books and having the technology there, we again reminded the leaders that reading is everywhere and how the library can supply what they need.

Publicity, Publicity, Publicity

Our "ask me about e-books" campaign began as a result of the dramatic increase in e-book checkout statistics we saw at the end of 2010. It was obvious that this new collection was taking off, but we still heard from patrons that some friends and neighbors didn't know the library offered e-book borrowing. We knew we had to get the word out further. This is what was done, both for our patrons and for library staff:

- We first turned to our traditional publicity methods: bookmarks, flyers, press releases, website, and a notice in the library's newsletter, all with the same logo and slogan—"Ask Me About eBooks."

- We added a very large banner to the outside of the buildings to catch drivers going by.

- We recently bought a button maker, so we made buttons for everyone on the staff to wear.

- Realizing that not everyone wearing a button would actually be able to answer confidently e-book-related questions, staff training became a must. A representative from our library system who had been trained by OverDrive came to our library and trained the librarians, who then could train the rest of the staff.

- Because training wasn't mandatory at the time, we knew it was only fair to provide a short, preprinted script that could be easily remembered if the staff members wearing the button but never got the training weren't confident in their answers about e-books.

Conclusion

E-books have brought to the library new attention from patrons who may have forgotten about us. There are members of our community who are visiting us virtually and reading our e-books whom we may

What Worked

We've seen an increase in awareness of the availability of e-books that can be borrowed from the library. We keep this awareness up with the petting zoo in the library and the regular Facebook posts and tweets that share news and articles from blogs and online newspapers and magazines.

What Didn't Work as Well

The Book Discussion Summit. We had a wonderful speaker and the group was lively, but trying to introduce the e-book format was intrusive. Participants wanted to talk books, not technology. I'd like to repeat the Book Discussion Summit but maybe focus on how to attract new members by keeping up with technology and have a speaker who can bring that subject alive. We are hoping that the new e-book users group will attract not only those interested in sharing tips about the technology but also those who want to talk about what they've read.

never meet in person. A great many are still coming in to check out print books, however. We need to serve both segments with the same enthusiasm and supply them with great reading and service.

Circulating E-Book Readers—Texas A&M University at Qatar

Carole Thompson

Example 3

Introduction

The library of Texas A&M University at Qatar began its trial of e-readers in May 2008 by ordering three of the leading brands available at that time, Sony Reader, iRex iLiad, and a first-generation Kindle. A major factor in the decision to deploy e-reader devices was the lack of physical shelf space, the high cost of shipping print materials, and the lengthy delays that occurred when shipping from the United States to Qatar. Limitations required that priority be reserved for academic titles, but interest in supplemental materials, such as bestselling fiction or nonfiction, was sufficient that an alternative delivery system merited experimenting with e-readers and electronic text. Readers, using devices for the first time, consistently expressed concern over the reading experience and focused their feedback on comparing reading on a device versus reading from printed text.

The available print book market in Qatar was extremely limited. Only one store sold current English language books and generally not current titles in academic or current released titles. The e-readers, if successful, would allow the library to quickly purchase, download, and circulate book requests to faculty, staff, and students. By purchasing electronic formats, there was no space commitment to nonpriority materials, saving precious shelf space for critical items available only in print. Another consideration was the cost of shipping interlibrary-loaned print books to and from the main campus of Texas A&M University in College Station, Texas, an expensive and time-consuming venture. Internally, the ease of purchase and maintenance of the e-readers would affect the library's decision of which e-reader to eventually deploy into our environment. Although located overseas, the network on the Qatar college campus is a U.S. IP range, allowing the library more freedom in its decisions when choosing titles available in electronic format.

The Readers

In 2008, the e-reader market was an emerging trend and the choices were limited. Amazon had released its first Kindle, Sony had offered its Reader, and the iRex iLiad was a European competitor. Over the first two years of the use of e-readers in the campus environment, this changed significantly, prompting many new models on the market and a much larger array of titles available for them in electronic format.

The iLiad

The iLiad was a slightly larger, more complex device, but overall the difficulty of locating titles for purchase among the several "bookstore" options and the problematic method of connecting the device to a personal computer made it a less attractive option. While the campus engineering faculty and students seemed to gravitate naturally toward this more fully featured, complex device and appreciated the USB connection that permitted reading .pdf documents directly off of USB-connected flash drives, the majority of our user population felt the basic operation was too slow, in particular, the device startup and page turning. The diversity of options and features did generate interest. For example, the font display could be set to 16 different sizes as opposed to the three or five sizes in the other devices. The built-in stylus allowed drawings that could be imported back to the user's computer. The iLiad was a very well-thought-out and well-engineered device, but the difficulty in simple, routine processes discouraged use.

The Kindle

The Kindle generated great interest and possibilities, but drawbacks due to the environment made it more problematic to manage. While the reading experience was consistently considered excellent by readers, the keyboard took too much space away from the reading screen and provided too little benefit. Feedback from end users raised this point consistently. From the perspective of managing a title library on the early Kindle device (first generation, 2008), the process of sorting titles on devices was problematic for library staff. After purchasing titles, a manual process to download and move titles onto the device was required (not so in more recent iterations of the management of the device), and the rights requirements were one title per device. This has since been much improved by Amazon and would not today be a factor if the decision was remade. Given the intense marketing of the device by Amazon, the device then and now enjoys the highest name recognition by readers, but the work involved in managing devices in a circulating library environment overcame our initial interest.

The Sony Reader

The Sony Reader was, by comparison, the obvious "consumer" device, well featured with fast startup, clear screens in digital ink, small and light for carrying, and a comfortable but brief selection of features such as only three font sizes. From the perspective of managing the device, the purchase of titles from the Sony bookstore was straightforward and simple, very similar to the way that music can be purchased, managed, and synced to devices using iTunes.

Implementation

Library staff concluded that the model best suited to the environment was the Sony Reader, and eventually several were purchased and maintained. Eventually, a larger inventory was required to substitute for models sent for repair or replacement, but the demand for e-books easily justified this. The work flow of maintaining the title library on each device was simpler to accomplish and less time-consuming, also providing simplicity in cataloging titles in the library's online catalog.

Content

Reading devices are a simple combination of hardware and application software. The real issue in implementing the e-readers as a service is the availability and delivery of the content. The core of this lies in the digital rights management (DRM) of purchased titles and how each content vendor had constructed its DRM model in relation to use of content on a device. Sony's bookstore permitted loading one purchased title onto six devices: one copy on the PC library and syncing of the title on up to five Sony Readers. By syncing all purchased titles to a "herd" of e-readers, the library staff circumvented the need to manage specific titles on specific readers. The regular procedure upon the return of a device was to charge and sync all current titles onto each device, making it ready for the next user. In other words, when a title was requested and purchased, it was loaded onto all e-reader devices, permitting all of our patrons to select from the full library of titles when checking out a device.

Work Flow

The purchase and loading process was very simple and fast. When a patron requested a title, a library staff member would open the Sony Bookstore and check for the title. If available, it was purchased, downloaded, and synced out to an available device and then charged out through a normal circulation process to the patron, also making the patron an active participant in the choice of materials available through the library (a form of patron-driven acquisition). Literally, this could be accomplished while the patron waited and in less time than it would take to walk to the shelves and locate a print volume in a more traditional setting.

The loan period the library settled on was two weeks. In the absence of a waiting list, a common occurrence, renewals of an e-reader were permitted. To reduce the waiting list, the library would also purchase titles, when available, and load them onto other devices such as a Kindle or iLiad, although this was not the preferred route. Unfortunately, some of the savvier reading public wanted to transfer content to their personal devices, but this was not possible. The current limitation of Kindle titles on Kindle devices or device application software versus having Sony titles only on Sony Readers is prohibitive and constraining. Ultimately, this turns title purchases into "throwaway" collections that will not carry forward as devices are replaced.

At the point that the Sony Reader software feature of collections was added, library staff developed genre collections so that nonfiction, mysteries, thrillers, and other areas of requested titles were subdivided to match interests. To some extent this would mimic a public library shelving scheme that divides genres of print books for easy browsing. The use of genres was duplicated from bestselling lists and reviews. In the case when a title might fit more than one genre, for instance, a science fiction/thriller, it could be added to each of the collections, as the title appearing in the collection folder was actually just a link to the single file in the e-reader library. The Sony Reader allowed the same kind of folder structure that iPod owners would see on their device. Each folder was the same as an iTunes playlist. While all files reside only in the main Library on the Reader, a user can create folders, name them for their genre, and drag a title into the folder. All that actually exists in the folder is a shortcut to the file located in the library. This is a simple but effective means of organizing.

The majority of requested titles are bestselling fiction, because of the initial lack of available nonfiction and academic titles. This began to change rapidly as sales increased and more current titles were published as digital content, allowing the library to develop and circulate a broader collection, with reduced cost and delay. Older titles published before the mid-1990s are rarely, if ever, available. Based on searching, titles published in the United States from the late-1990s onward are quite often available, but foreign published titles, non-English language, or academic titles are equally unavailable. During the initial experience, it appeared that the electronic version of a title becomes available approximately six weeks after the print version is released.

Over the course of three years, the library continued to buy additional readers, develop an upkeep procedure for sending broken devices back to Sony for exchange or repair, and expand device capacity by adding 2 GB flash memory cards to the readers, permitting the increase from 160 titles per device up to 1,500 or more titles. Some of the original e-readers have been cycled out in favor of the newer models, some of which have the built-in light, although this feature reduces the quality of the digital ink display and may be preferred or not preferred by the end users. To some extent the variety of models is less attractive, but this does not inhibit the use of the devices by those who use them. Individuals have developed preferences for specific models, although there does seem to be a preference for the newer devices that feature touch screens.

The newest device being trialed as a reading device is the Apple iPad. Although very different in nature because of the diverse applications it supports, the initial use of various reading software, such as iBook from

Apple, Kindle for iPad, or the Barnes & Noble Nook, has been met with increasing interest and acceptance. It is currently being trialed in a film class, using both textbooks in electronic format and films for students to watch and analyze. The infectious spread of electronic readers, iPads, smartphones, and other "smart" devices was bound to spill into the curricula at some point. By piloting the devices, it gave the library, faculty, students, and other university support staff an opportunity to experiment before making the more extensive commitment to trialing in a classroom setting.

Conclusion

The overall experience has demonstrated that our reading public continues to enjoy a variety of electronic publications on continually evolving devices. As for library staff, the preference would be to have many more titles in many more types of genres available using these technologies and to have more flexibility in purchasing a standard format so as not to limit what titles could be loaded on which device. Our preference would be to have the ability to move titles purchased from one vendor onto devices sold by other vendors, particularly as devices evolve and earlier models are replaced.

Hopefully, the market will not only deepen and broaden the content available in electronic content but also be standardized on specific EPUB formats that will allow transfer much the way PDF files can be read on almost every kind of computer or device. Consumers will likely hone their preferences, and this will be a catalyzing factor in market development, as demands for particular devices and ease of use convinces publishers to produce content in response. And the consumers themselves will exert their preferences by purchasing devices and content. It seems likely that a library such as this will revert to delivering content rather than technology, as a model such as OverDrive gains in popularity. In the meantime, the library enjoys the compliments of satisfied readers who appreciate the service and continue to rely on it but will no doubt evolve the program as the market of e-readers and electronic content changes.

Changing Library Staffing Models to Manage E-Collections—George Washington University

Kathe S. Obrig

Example 4

Introduction

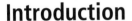

The Himmelfarb Health Sciences Library at George Washington University migrated to a journal and book collection that was increasingly electronic in scope; it realized that it had to fundamentally reassess how the collections department was organized. The collections department performs activities specific to print and electronic collection development, ordering and preparation for all resources, cataloging, and systems and all maintenance tasks for existing collections. This E-Books in Practice example will examine the process that the library underwent to revise job tasks, work flow, and job descriptions in order to adjust to the growing electronic landscape.

Changing Collection Formats— Changing Staffing Needs

From 2005 to 2011, our electronic book collection grew from 70 titles to slightly over 600. We also converted all of our core journal titles (over 1,000 titles) to electronic access only and have overall access to approximately 2,800 e-journals titles.

With the substantial increase of resources in electronic format, we soon found that the changes in activities required to support and maximize usability resulted in a shift in the tasks performed by staff. At the same time as the electronic materials grew in volume, the number of print materials reduced significantly each year, requiring fewer and fewer of the tasks associated with print maintenance. With the shift in tasks, the skills that staff had used in a more print-rich environment were not necessarily the same skills now required. In some cases, individuals had taken on tasks in previous years because they excelled at or had experience that was no longer pertinent to the activities or the work flow that was now required.

IN THIS CHAPTER:

✔ Introduction

✔ Changing Collection Formats— Changing Staffing Needs

✔ Resulting Organizational Changes

✔ Successful Implementation

✔ Conclusion

In late 2008, a mandated move of approximately 65,000 bound print journals from the library's second floor and the conversion of that area entirely to student study space meant that many more print journals would either be transferred to an off-site facility or be housed in on-site storage in a lower level; all binding would cease when the current year's materials were bound; and electronic backfiles would replace the print bound volumes as the budget permitted. The time for the library to reorganize to better reflect the changing nature of its collections had arrived.

Staff Reorganization—New Skills Required

One caveat that the library had to work under was that there would be no opportunity to modify the overall organizational structure in the area; the full-time equivalents had to remain as they were, although job descriptions and work responsibilities could be changed. Nine staff members totaling eight full-time equivalent (seven full-time plus two half-time) positions were to be involved in the organizational job conversion effort. Achieving successful reorganization required buy-in from all staff affected. To elicit the perspective and input of all involved, the staff took an afternoon to go on a "retreat" off-site to focus totally on the need for reorganization.

Managing Electronic Resources

At the retreat, the staff identified the observed changes needing translation into position modifications as follows:

- More options for purchasing materials exist with electronic resources (use of an aggregator, direct from publisher, individual title, package, etc.), raising the complexity of decision making and requiring changes in acquisitions work flow and collection development decisions.

- Commitment to maintaining collection integrity with print items no longer preserved on the shelf required new methods of archiving and perpetual access such as Portico and LOCKSS.

- Mastering increased and different types of license agreements and their individual internal properties (reading, negotiating, tracking, implementing, and compliance with) was time-consuming in multiple departments and required a steep learning curve.

- The decision to provide direct links for access from the library homepage and catalog and full-text access directly to content from within bibliographic databases required new or modified work flows as well as synchronization between them.

- Increased user training and library technical support was required to assist users in successfully using e-resources and to troubleshoot technical problems with resource access, including proxy and other off-campus use issues. Sometimes this was just a learning curve issue for the user, while other issues required contact with the publisher or vendor to correct access problems.

- Additional record-keeping was required, as the integrated library system was unable to keep track of the types of information needed for e-resources. Recording of the troubleshooting of access concerns was also desired, and the library subsequently purchased an electronic resource management system to deal with these issues. But staff to maintain this new system still was required.

- Increased time was required to accomplish the interlibrary loan function because of use of an increased number of systems and greater complexity with electronic resources.

- Individuals needed to interact more frequently with the library homepage/webmaster because of the library's decision to provide full-text access points to book and journal resources on the homepage and to accomplish tasks that became increasingly web based. The fact that the webmaster worked in a different area and physical location required liaison duties to be added for adequate communication and effective operations.

- More systems were required to manage e-resources than print, increasing time to maintain each.

- Additional cataloging time was required for new multitype resources.

Managing Print Resources

While increasing electronic resources directly impacts work flow and job descriptions, most libraries still maintain print collections and still need staff to manage these collections. Some of these tasks' workloads have diminished, but others have been eliminated, such as the binding operation. The following are tasks still needed in today's e-library:

- Print journal processing tasks are diminishing in volume but still need to be accomplished on a smaller scale.

- Print book ordering and invoicing as well as the physical preparation of all monographic materials continues to exist.

- Print reserves decreased with the increased ability for electronic reserves within Blackboard.

Resulting Organizational Changes

As a result of the retreat and the analysis of changing work flow and skill sets, the following organizational changes occurred:

- The serials librarian position was retained as a separate full-time position from that of the part-time electronic resources librarian, who manages only electronic books and databases. The serials librarian and a full-time support person were needed to devote their time solely to electronic serials acquisition and maintenance duties. All three positions needed to increase collaboration and communication to make for a successful e-resources management team. The cataloging librarian position remained largely unchanged, although the complexity had increased and more time was required to accomplish the functional needs. Some smaller tasks were shifted to other positions to increase available cataloging time.

- The print collections librarian continued to focus on the acquisition and maintenance of print resources only but now actively collaborates with the electronic resources librarian regarding building the collection of both print and electronic book materials.

- The systems librarian remained a half-time position because of organizational budgetary constraints. The increased systems-related tasks, aside from maintenance of the integrated library system, were distributed to the specific area most affected (e.g., management of the electronic resource management system became a duty of the serials department, interlibrary loan managed its own systems, etc.).

- Each position had tasks added reflecting new activities specific to electronic resources.

- The support position that previously processed book ordering and other similar tasks assumed management of the interlibrary loan process in addition to other database maintenance and collection coordination tasks.

- The former bindery assistant position was totally repurposed to focus on print functions such as ordering and maintenance of all types of print materials for both serials and books.

- The increased communication and collaboration across areas to ensure that each book or journal title (both print and electronic) was fully deployed and maintained was reflected in each job description.

- Each position is responsible for any needed interface of its area with the webmaster.

- Each position was re-titled to reflect new focus and updated responsibilities.

Successful Implementation

The whole process of organizational redesign was very intensive, complex, and time-consuming. Participation of each individual in detailing current duties and identifying changes was pivotal to the success of the effort, because only the individual actually performing the job could know how involved each step was and the approximate amount of time needed to accomplish each task. Most of the changed and increased activities required development of new skills or increased learning curves. Various methods were identified (courses, webinars, staff instructing staff, etc.) to increase expertise. Further experience and education in the copyright area has been required in multiple positions. The large-scale change toward e-resources collections has also modified the budget process. As an example, staff spends more time in internal accounting duties to better track the individual types of materials purchased and cost, in anticipation of the time when the university makes the budget process more reflective of current purchasing practices. Maintaining open communication and collaboration on an ongoing basis and individual accountability for its success have helped ensure that the process worked. We feel the new organization more effectively supports the needs of our users within the environment of new technology advances.

Conclusion

The review and reassessment of the technical positions within collections proved to be a valuable use of staff time and resulted in needed position modifications. Subsequent evaluation of the reorganization process showed that it worked well for the library's specific internal situation and could be used again. An important aspect of the evaluation process was having individual input regarding the time required for accomplishment of each duty; this proved pivotal in making appropriate position decisions. The needed budgetary modifications continue to be reflected in internal accounting changes annually, but the overall changes to the budgeting methodology of the university to better reflect the current allocation of expenditures continue to be anticipated. While this position review did not include any modifications of the overall organizational structure within collections (number and distribution of full-time positions required), future reviews will consider this aspect. The collections area has determined that this type of position review should occur at approximately three-year intervals to ensure maximal function of the area. As of this writing, the library has just embarked on another review, which will be conducted using the same process.

E-Book Access Management Using an ERM System— Oregon Health & Science University

Kristina DeShazo

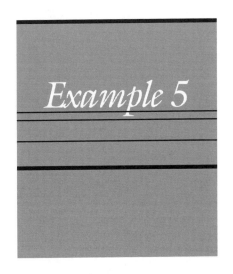

Example 5

Introduction

In all libraries, the mantra of timeliness, accuracy, and completeness weighs in every interaction with users. Perhaps nowhere is it felt more keenly than when meeting the needs of the medical community where rapid dissemination of information can literally have life and death consequences. Managing access to electronic materials to meet those needs has come a long way over the past decade. As electronic resources grew in number and complexity, new products were developed to make them available alongside traditional print resources. This E-Books in Practice example will describe how one library implemented an electronic resource management (ERM) system that now makes e-books available to its population.

E-Resources at OHSU

The Oregon Health & Science University (OHSU) Library began providing links to electronic journals through a simple HTML page of links in 1998. The A to Z list included e-journals for which publishers granted access to any subscriber of the print publication. Thus began the tedious task of gathering the information title-by-title either through correspondence with the publisher or searching journal websites. Over time, as collections of journals grew and became available from large aggregators, it was obvious that a new system would be needed to make these resources accessible to library patrons. To tackle this problem, OHSU Library developed a relational database (SQL) backend with ColdFusion used for the webpage interface. SQL is a structured query language, or programming language designed to query a database. For the most part this solved the issue of updating and maintaining links.

In 2003, we considered the developing market for electronic holdings management systems, including EBSCO A-to-Z, Serials Solutions, and TDNet, but found a lack of integration with the online catalog and the inability to provide multiple links per title. After careful review, we stayed with our SQL database, which offered more flexibility and provided the necessary multiple link capability. However, lack of integration with the catalog system meant two problems remained: (1) searching in two different systems to find electronic resources and (2) duplication of data entry. Having a separate database from the catalog meant an individual looking for a particular journal title would have to search both the catalog and the A to Z webpage to find out whether we owned a title in print or had electronic access. Simultaneously, electronic access had been made available from the catalog for many journals. Therefore, updating the SQL database meant the catalog also needed updating.

Electronic resource management (ERM) systems began to emerge in 2004 from a variety of vendors including integrated library system (ILS) providers. OHSU Library was presented with the opportunity to become a beta tester for the Innovative Interfaces Inc.'s Electronic Resources Management (ERM) module. The new product had the advantage of being an add-on module to our ILS and included a link resolver. Link resolvers provide links among databases, allowing systems to transmit data and connect from one part of one system to one part of another system where that information syncs up. With the added incentive of a discount for the ERM module and the opportunity to influence its development, we decided to join as beta testers.

ERM—Development and Implementation

OHSU Library is a medium-sized academic health sciences library with a staff of fewer than 40 full- and part-time individuals. A cross-departmental team was assembled pulling individuals from cataloging and systems departments as well as acquisitions, public services, and reference. Everyone had a stake in the end result and felt compelled to be in on the project. As beta testers we provided feedback on features and functions as they were made available to us by Innovative Interfaces and used test loads to put the module through its paces. Over several months a resource record was created for each provider of content with data about the provider. A license record was also created and held data specific to the license agreement for each set of titles from the provider. Contact records included names of sales representatives as well as technical support contact information. And finally holdings were loaded from the SQL database to the coverage database included in the module. Five years later we continue to use the Innovative Interfaces module and manage well over 300 resource records with holdings. That is not to say everything works in perfect concert with no issues. There are many extenuating circumstances over which we have no control and continue to work through them as they arise. Issues come in the form of poor title and holdings lists from publishers and difficulties in representing title changes over time when access is linked under only the current title. Users experiencing these breaks in the linkages become frustrated and just assume that we do not have those titles or that the system does not work, or both. These are but two of the larger problems that have seen some degree of resolution, although there is still much work to be done.

ERM—From E-Journal Management to E-Book Management

At OHSU, we are witnessing the same evolution of issues and concerns that occurred with e-journals as we move forward in making e-books available through our catalog. The process of adding an individual e-journal or e-book remains relatively the same as for print. And, as with e-journals, handling a package or collection of e-books presents problems of quantity and quality. While we are thrilled to be able to provide access to a large number of titles, the sheer volume can be daunting. Using the ERM module helps manage integration of these title sets into the catalog, providing the user one interface for searching library materials. At the heart of the ERM is the resource record that identifies the source of the electronic content. Bibliographic records are linked to the holding record, which obtains the link data on the fly from the coverage database. The holding record is soft linked to the resource record. Publisher title lists continue to be problematic, and, where holdings statement accuracy was an issue for electronic journals, for electronic books obtaining quality MARC records particularly for packages or collections of e-books presents a new set of issues. As with e-journals before, third-party vendors including Serials Solutions and SFX have begun to provide holdings management services for e-books. At present, OHSU Library continues to manage holdings by obtaining title list and MARC record sets from publishers. And, where available, we have utilized the services of OCLC's WorldCat Cataloging Partners to obtain MARC records. The latter are especially helpful to us as they contain the necessary bibliographic data to aid the discovery of our content in our consortial catalog.

The difficulties of implementation and maintenance continue to challenge us as the volume of electronic resources grows. The multitude of relevant resources has been daunting, as announcements of new publisher platforms and content are evident on a regular basis. Still, we strive to stay focused on our goal of providing one-stop-shopping for electronic resources to our users. With each announcement of new platforms we must investigate the method of access. We find ourselves in the position of educating content providers regarding search and discovery and the benefits of making their content discoverable in the already established catalog in addition to their own platform. Additionally, rather than working with third-party holdings management services we have chosen to work in smaller batches, one publisher at a time. This may not be an option for a larger organization with a wider scope of resources to maintain.

It truly does "take a village" to acquire, set up, and maintain electronic resources. The implementation process and management requires a concerted effort across at least a couple of departmental lines no matter how the library is organized. For many organizations this in itself is the stumbling block. First, a trial of a new package of titles or platform may take place before the decision to buy. This may require the skills of technical services individuals to make the content accessible and available from the library website. Negotiation of the content to be included or certain license terms may be required and could include individuals from acquisitions, collection management, or public services. Once the purchase decision is made the order process is essentially the same as for any print material handled by acquisitions. The next step in the process is cataloging, followed by gathering holdings or link data. The latter step may be accomplished by the cataloger or access management assistants. While this sounds very linear, in reality the process can be more jumbled. Sometimes the title lists received in the negotiation process include all the holding and link data necessary to add content to the ERM, which will create a brief bibliographic record in the load process. Of course, these lack metadata essential to discovery in the catalog, which is why we prefer to obtain full MARC records before loading link data.

Staffing Changes Needed to Maintain an ERM System

At OHSU Library positions evolved to manage electronic resources. The electronic journals librarian position expanded with serials acquisitions responsibilities for both print and electronic journals. Later acquisition for all material types including print and electronic books was added, and finally acknowledgment of electronic resources management duties was added to the position description. As for other positions, the collection development support position helped in the initial setup of resource records and license records. Later, that position took on most of the day-to-day maintenance activities for e-journals. Cataloging of e-journals began with one individual handling the cataloging. Packages and collections became more prevalent, and all available cataloging assistants helped manage the workload even as we continued to purchase about the same number of print monographs. The reduction of print journal subscriptions did free up some serials assistant time to help with day-to-day electronic resource management such as audits and holdings maintenance. While this may sound like everyone simply got more work to do, the reality is that we could not have done this work without the ERM system. We have been able to reduce staff time on managing electronic resources as the system and our processes have improved.

ERM—Moving Forward

For OHSU Library using the ERM to manage e-book access was an extension of a system already in place for e-journals. Adjustments were made in processes to accommodate the few differences involved, particularly with regard to collections of titles. Much of the hard work of setting up the ERM system was behind us. What served us best was a concerted effort to define the process and responsibilities along the work flow. We continue to work on refining the process and have found that a certain amount of flexibility is necessary, as not every resource fits neatly into the work flow. What works for us may not work exactly the same way for another organization. Each library must develop its own process work flow to serve its own needs. Libraries considering implementation of an ERM system today will have the benefit of learning from those that have gone before. User groups and electronic discussion lists as well as publications such as this one are available where they were not when we were first venturing into electronic resource management. One interesting resource begun in 2011 is the *TERMS: Techniques for ER Management* community blog at http://6terms.tumblr.com/ where all libraries are encouraged to share their work flow processes for the benefit of all.

Conclusion

Many libraries are still considering implementing an ERM but are daunted by the time needed to translate work flow into database fields and the time needed to populate and maintain the system. As electronic resources overtake print collections in most libraries, the question is not should we have an ERM but which system should be purchased and how to get started. Proper management of our electronic resources is not only essential for selection, budgeting, licensing, and technical processing, but also for reliable user access.

Accessing and Circulating E-Books with E-Readers— Lesley University

Marilyn Geller and Linda Roscoe

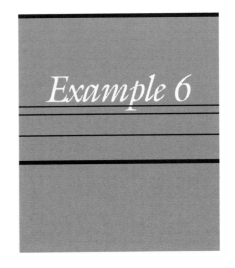

Example 6

Background

Sherrill Library is the main library at Lesley University, a small university with an enrollment of about 4,000 in Cambridge, Massachusetts, which specializes in teacher training and expressive therapies. In the spring of 2010, funds were made available for a pilot project to introduce e-book readers (e-readers) to the community. The purposes of the pilot were to:

- promote use of the comprehensive e-book collections available through the library,
- encourage patrons to become familiar with new technology and publishing formats, and
- test alternative methods of delivering content to patrons.

E-Reader Selection

Sherrill Library acquired one Sony PRS-600 and one iPad model A1219. There are a number of devices on the market that could be purchased, but we had money for only two. In some ways, it was an arbitrary decision. Our reasoning in selecting the iPad was that it seemed to be more than a simple reading device and would give our patrons opportunities to explore more than just e-books. At the time planning was begun, the library's acquisition policy prevented us from ordering through Amazon, thus eliminating the Kindle as an option. After some research, the two librarians assigned to this project selected the Sony Reader as our second trial device.

The initial budget for the project was $299 to $500 for the Sony, $499 to $699 for the iPad, and $200 for content to be divided between the two devices. Because Apple and Sony do not allow purchase orders or vouchers to be used, gift cards that the university reimbursed were acquired. These were used at the Sony Reader store and the Apple iTunes store to purchase books. Apps for the iPad were also purchased using the same gift card.

Selecting Content

Several decisions were made about content, including selection of materials, purchase of materials, and loading of materials. Our selection process was guided by the same principles we use in acquiring materials for the New & Noteworthy and Casual Collections. These collections include both fiction and nonfiction for general and pleasure reading. The intent in selecting these types of materials was to focus on the issue of readability on the devices. Titles that were selected and purchased were then loaded onto the appropriate devices. The library staff tried to solicit recommendations for content from users via a paper survey included with the reading devices and on the E-Reader LibGuide (Lesley University Library, 2010) with the intention of accommodating requests within the parameters of the content budget and standard selection criteria for the New & Noteworthy and Casual Collections. Although the survey provided some feedback on the ease of use of each device, users did not suggest additional content. A more aggressive approach is now being planned in which circulation staff will insert flyers into books being checked out. These flyers will say "I'd like to read _____ on the _____ device."

Access Decisions

Several decisions were also made with respect to technical processing, including whether and how to catalog the devices and titles on the devices and how to package and process the physical devices. We created the item type E-READER for the library's OPAC. Because we wanted to highlight not only the device but also the content loaded on the device, catalog records were created for each device with contents notes listing each author and title and with added entries that would bring catalog searchers to the E-READER record if they searched for a book by title. To date, we have not created content notes or added entries for apps that have been loaded on the iPad. Our current thinking is that users won't be using the OPAC to search for these apps.

The Sony Reader was purchased with a protective sleeve, and a protective sleeve was separately purchased for the iPad. Each device had a bar code attached on the back. There was a good deal of discussion about special packaging for the devices and their associated paraphernalia, including connecting cables and wires, a laminated instruction sheet, a contents card, and the user survey. In the end, we used red plastic book pouches already in our supply collection and generally used for packaging Teaching Resources Kits; no special packaging was purchased for the e-reader devices.

Access decisions focused on loan periods, holds, fines, user agreements, and surveys. We initially decided to create a two-week loan period with no renewals. However, halfway through the fall semester, the waiting time became very long, particularly for the iPad. We changed the loan period to one week and now have more manageable waiting times.

As much as possible, we have tried to treat the e-reader devices like other items in the library collection that can be borrowed. However, we felt that because the devices were expensive, they deserved an extra measure of protection. To this end, a simple user agreement was created for borrowers to sign prior to checking devices out. This agreement spells out costs associated with late returns and damages as well as what happens to content loaded by the borrower, which is treated as a donation to the library. It also requires the patron's signature. As part of this agreement, we asked patrons to return the devices directly to staff at the circulation desk. This safeguarded the devices in some way, but it also allowed us to ask borrowers about their experiences with each device. Because we were not always certain that we would be able to capture this information, we included a very short survey in the packaging.

E-Reader Lending Research—Advice from Other Libraries

Fortunately, other academic libraries have initiated e-reader lending programs and were willing to share information. A Fairleigh Dickinson University librarian offered a helpful presentation on survey questions for users (O'Shea, 2010). Penn State Libraries has a useful tip sheet for using the Sony (Penn State University Libraries, 2011). In an e-mail communication with the authors and others, Holli Moseman of Indiana State University conducted an unpublished iPad survey and shared results with respondents. "The Kindle Initiative at Bryant" was presented at the ACRL/NEC Conference, May 14, 2010 (Crawford and Bond, 2010). "Lending Kindle E-Book Readers: First Results from the Texas A&M University Project" (Clark, 2009) was helpful as background information. Macalester College was a very good resource for creating our user agreement, although it is no longer accessible online.

Procedures for Checking in E-Readers

We created a two-stage maintenance procedure that allows circulation desk staff to accept a returning device and quickly verify that all parts are present and in working order. The second stage of this procedure is to have one of two certified staff members review all the content to make certain that everything that is supposed to be there is present and anything that was added is either deleted or accepted as a donation and left on the device. Each device is reset to its original borrowing condition and, when necessary, fully charged.

Introducing E-Readers to Library Staff

Soon after the devices were purchased and loaded we offered a "Show and Tell" session to the library staff. We explained the background of the project, the loan periods, and the check-in and checkout procedures. We also allowed people in groups to work with the devices and explore together. Then we made the devices available for borrowing by our student staff. The goal was to get them comfortable with each device so that they could advise patrons. We found that the student workers were quite interested and already adept in their use.

Marketing

The final set of activities centered on marketing. We felt that a large-scale marketing campaign might result in too many requests for the two devices, which could create a negative impression. Instead we chose a soft marketing campaign that only advertised the availability of these devices in places, both physical and virtual, where users come to us. The marketing plan included signage in the library itself, messages on the library's Facebook page, a notice in the News box on the myLibrary tab in the university's course management system, and the previously mentioned E-Reader LibGuide. Later on, physical book dummies were created for the titles loaded on the devices and placed on prominent display in our New & Noteworthy bookcase. With all of this accomplished, we began lending the two e-book devices during the 2010 fall semester and saw immediate interest from our patrons.

Lessons Learned

Although it has been only one and a half semesters since beginning to loan the e-reader devices, a great deal has already been learned from the results of our survey, from conversations with users, and from our own experiences:

- We have become more adept at handling the maintenance of each device and have discovered that the Sony is best recharged by being plugged into a computer, while the iPad is more efficiently charged via an electrical outlet.

- Expensive accessories are not necessary. The bags that we used for other library items worked just fine for containing the devices, their accessories, a tip sheet, and a user survey.

- The iPad is more popular than the Sony Reader. It is certainly perceived as capable of more than the Sony is. Furthermore, patrons have been willing to wait a few weeks to use the iPad. Among the possible uses for the iPad, users listed checking e-mail, reading news on the web, or as a kind of replacement for a laptop. One faculty member said she would use the iPad for reading PDF-formatted articles, student work, and documents related to meetings.

- There have been very few suggestions for additional titles, but several users have asked for additional apps. In response to that, we loaded two requested apps for the iPad (Pages and British Library: Treasures) and plan to load others.

- Even though the iPad has been more popular, some users found things they didn't like about it, and others found that they had a good or better experience with the Sony. One survey respondent said that the iPad was "very good for video, although heavy. O.K. as a web browser, but too heavy really. Not great for reading—screen reflection and too heavy, clunky." On the other hand, according to our users, the Sony was comfortable to read on, a bit lighter, easier to hang onto, and easier to "pop out" for a quick read on the bus or subway. The iPad was the opposite but was a much more useful device because of its ability to access the Internet. One person found the iPad heavy and slippery to use and would want a cover for it.

- Some users tried to extrapolate their experiences to use in the academic research environment. Five people said they could envision using an e-reader for Reserve readings, while others wondered how useful it could be for "work" reading and academic titles. While we were intrigued by this idea, we are currently focused on providing leisure reading on these devices. We also decided not to remove any device from general circulation by devoting it exclusively to Reserves.

Conclusion

Based on the broader popularity of the iPad and on the waiting times patrons are currently experiencing, we originally thought that Sherrill Library could purchase another iPad in the next budget year. On further consideration, we decided that we wanted to give our users the broadest possible range of device experiences and would like to consider purchasing either a Barnes & Noble Nook or an Amazon Kindle or both to add to our collection. With more devices available, we also want to consider how to market this initiative more widely. We would also like to find a more effective way to solicit suggestions for content and apps before a user borrows a device so that we can deliver what the user is most interested in working with on the device.

This pilot project was so successful that we no longer view it as an experiment. Our users have shown a definite interest in exploring these devices for use in both personal and professional areas, and we will continue to serve this need for them.

References

Clark, Dennis T. 2009. "Lending Kindle E-Book Readers: First Results from the Texas A&M University Project." *Collection Building* 28, no. 4: 146–149.

Crawford, Pat, and Jennifer Bond. 2010. "The Kindle Initiative at Bryant." Paper presented at ACRL/NEC Conference, May 14. College of the Holy Cross, Worcester, MA.

Lesley University Library. 2010. "E-Book Readers." Lesley University Library. http://research.lesley.edu/e-book_readers.

O'Shea, Denise. 2010. "eBooks, eReaders and Their Impact on Libraries." SlideShare. http://www.slideshare.net/denoshea/ebooks-ereaders-and.

Penn State University Libraries. 2011. "Sony Reader 101." Library Learning Services. http://www.libraries.psu.edu/psul/lls/sony_reader/sony_reader_use.html.

About the Editor and Contributors

About the Editor

Richard Kaplan is the Dean of Library and Learning Resources at the Massachusetts College of Pharmacy and Health Sciences. He has overseen the conversion of the College library and two branch campus libraries into a predominantly electronic collection. Rich has over 30 years of experience also working in libraries at Rensselaer Polytechnic Institute, the Massachusetts Institute of Technology, and the University of Buffalo (SUNY). He has an MLS from the University of Albany (SUNY) and has published in the *Journal of the Medical Library Association*, *Medical Reference Services Quarterly*, and the *Journal of Library Administration*. He can be reached at richard.kaplan@mcphs.edu.

About the Contributors

Becky Albitz has been the Electronic Resources Librarian at the Pennsylvania State University since 2001. She received her BA in Film and English from the University of Rochester, an MA in Film from Penn State, and her MLS from the University of Pittsburgh. She is currently working toward her doctorate in higher education from Penn State. Her publications on media, licensing, and copyright have appeared in a variety of venues, including *Portal, The Journal of Academic Librarianship, Collection Development*, and *The Acquisitions Librarian*. Becky also has given numerous presentations and workshops on copyright, licensing issues, and electronic books, including co-teaching the ARL online licensing course. Her book *Licensing and Managing Electronic Resources* was published in June 2008 by Chandos Press. She can be reached at rsa4@psu.edu.

David Brennan is the Collection Development/Digital Resources Management Librarian at the Pennsylvania State College of Medicine, Penn State Hershey. He has his MLS from the University of Pittsburgh. Mr. Brennan is currently responsible for policy creation and the evaluation, promotion, and management of all print, electronic, and media information resources with specific responsibility for developing policies, procedures, best practices, and documentation for managing the life cycle of electronic resources. He leads the Collection Development Team, supervises the operations of the Collection Access and Support Unit, and administers the Harrell Health Sciences Library's collection budget. In previous positions, Mr. Brennan has also been a health sciences library director and a systems librarian with responsibilities for both collection development and overall library management. He can be reached at dbrennan@hmc.psu.edu.

Fern M. Cheek is an Assistant Professor and Research Librarian at The Ohio State University, Health Sciences Library. She has an AMLS degree from the University of Michigan and has worked in health sciences libraries for 35 years both in the hospital libraries and the academic library. Fern has had experience in the areas of acquisitions, collection development, and comprehensive database searching. Currently, her role as research librarian involves working with those involved in biomedical and health sciences research to identify resources and strategies in doing comprehensive literature reviews as well as being a team member for systematic review. She can be reached at fern.cheek@osumc.edu.

Tom Corbett holds an MLIS from the University of Missouri, supplemented by many years of continuing education in informational technologies. He has worn many hats over his 30-year career, from assistant director of an urban public library to systems librarian for a mixed-library consortium. His most recent challenge as Library Director of the Fisher-Watkins Library has been to develop the digital library at Cushing Academy, a private preparatory school in New England, after the administrators made the bold and controversial decision to "go bookless" with their library in 2009. He can be reached at tcorbett@cushing.org.

Kristina DeShazo received her MLS from Emporia State University and has been with Oregon Health & Science University Library in Portland, Oregon, since 2002. Her duties and job title expanded to Acquisitions & E-Resources Librarian in 2009 when duties in electronic resource acquisitions, maintenance, and support, including development of effective work flows and procedures, were recognized. She can be reached at deshazok@ohsu.edu.

Joanne Doucette is Head of Collections & Technical/Access Services at the Massachusetts College of Pharmacy and Health Sciences in Boston, Massachusetts. She received her MS in Library and Information Science from Simmons College. Her position includes selecting, ordering, and processing e-books and other library resources in the health sciences. Joanne can be reached at joanne.doucette@mcphs.edu.

Ellen Druda is the Internet Services Librarian at the Half Hollow Hills Community Library in Dix Hills, New York. She has her MLS from the Palmer School of Library and Information Science at Long Island University. She is currently working on engaging patrons with e-book readers through users groups and a petting zoo and hoping to move past the technology and get them reading and sharing tips and ideas with each other in their own book discussion group. Ellen can be reached at edruda@suffolk.lib.ny.us.

Betsy Eggleston is the Director of Collections & Knowledge Management at the Francis A. Countway Library of Medicine, Harvard Medical School. She received her MSLS from Simmons College in 1985. She is formerly Head of Harvard College Library/ Faculty of Arts and Sciences (HCL/FAS) Cataloging Support Service and has been involved in cataloging for most of her career. In her current position, she orders hundreds of e-books and works with staff to ensure that they are cataloged efficiently and readily available to the user. Elizabeth can be reached at elizabeth_eggleston@hms.harvard.edu.

Rebecca Felkner is the Assistant Director of the Grandview Heights Public Library, Columbus, Ohio. Previously she was a Library Consultant at the State Library of Ohio and Program Officer of the Library and Information Technology Association at the American Library Association in addition to working as a reference librarian in academic and special libraries. As Library Consultant at the State Library of Ohio, she managed the Ohio eBook Project consortium from its inception in 2005 until September 2008, led public libraries through long-range planning processes, and managed the statewide interlibrary loan system for Ohio public libraries. Ms. Felkner earned her MLS degree from Kent State University. She can be reached at rfelkner@ghpl.org.

Marilyn Geller is the Collection Management Librarian for the Lesley University Library in Cambridge, Massachusetts, where her responsibilities include collection development and digital services support. Ms. Geller began her professional library career as a cataloger at the Tozzer Library at Harvard University and later became a serials cataloger at the Massachusetts Institute of Technology Libraries. Ms. Geller went on to work for Readmore, Inc., a wholly owned subsidiary of Blackwell's Information Services, where she was responsible for Internet product development. She also spent several years as an independent consultant and was involved in a variety of projects for subscription agencies, service providers, publishers, nonprofit organizations, and libraries. One of these projects was to act as project manager for Harvard University's Mellon grant to explore e-journal archiving. Ms. Geller was awarded an MLS from Simmons College in 1978. She can be reached at mgeller@lesley.edu.

Karen S. Grigg is the Associate Director of Collection Development Services at Duke Medical Center Library. She oversees selection and acquisitions of the library's book collection and databases and provides analysis of the use of the collection. Before working at Duke, she was the Textiles and Engineering Services Librarian at North Carolina State University Libraries. Karen received her MSLS in 1998 at University of North Carolina at Chapel Hill. In order to provide a more data-driven collection development environment, Karen led efforts to analyze use of both print and electronic books and to identify unique ways in which libraries can determine the efficacy of e-book purchasing decisions and has co-presented posters and papers on this topic previous to authoring this chapter. She can be reached at karen.grigg@duke.edu.

Lynda J. Hartel is Associate Director of the Health Sciences Library and Assistant Professor at The Ohio State University. For many years, Lynda managed library collection development, acquisitions, and cataloging operations. She is now charged with leading knowledge integration efforts in the library and in forming and working with strategic partnerships across the OSU Campus and Medical Center. She is a member of the Medical Library Association and the Healthcare Information and Management Systems Society. Lynda holds an MLS from Emporia State University and has published and presented in the areas of collection development, open access publishing, and consumer health. Fern Cheek and Lynda coauthored the article "Preferred Book Formats in an Academic Medical Center," *Journal of the Medical Library Association*, October 2011, 99(4): 313–317, which discusses different customers (students, faculty, and staff) and their preferences for obtaining information found in books. E-books and print books were the focus of the study. She can be reached at lynda.hartel@osumc.edu.

Nadia J. Lalla is a graduate of McGill University where she received her MLIS degree. She is currently the Coordinator of Collections and Information Services at the Taubman Health Sciences Library, University of Michigan. In this position, she manages staff and activities focused on the delivery of reference services (in person and virtual) and the design and implementation of instructional technologies. As the Collections Coordinator, Nadia selects print and electronic resources in the health sciences disciplines, including licensing negotiations with major biomedical vendors. Nadia has nearly 25 years of experience in the field of librarianship, including all aspects of reference, instruction, and collection management. She has worked in a variety of settings from academe and nonprofit organizations to public and special libraries. Nadia's experiences have propelled her to participate in the transition from a primarily print milieu to an overwhelmingly digital library environment. She can be reached at nadiamar@umich.edu.

Amy Lewontin is the Collection Development Librarian at Northeastern University in Boston. Her responsibilities include planning and management of collection development, including collaboration with subject collection managers in all discipline-related projects. She is involved in implementing a new patron-driven acquisitions program for STM books and analyzes the collections for usage, accreditation standards, and budget. In addition, she evaluates and trials new electronic resources and has developed and implemented a library-wide collection assessment program. As Cochair of the Collection Development Interest Group ACRL/New England Chapter she has planned two programs: E-Books: A Brief Fix on a Moving Target and The Book: The Rumors of My Death Have Been Greatly Exaggerated. Amy has her MLS from Simmons College. She can be reached at a.lewontin@neu.edu.

Kathe S. Obrig is Associate Director of Collections and Access Services for Himmelfarb Health Sciences Library of the George Washington University. Kathe received her MLS from Western Michigan University. Her current position involves management of both the traditional technical services and circulation departments. She has been extensively involved in a number of review and reorganization efforts for the Collections Department of the Himmelfarb Library due to the many external and internal environmental changes since assuming her current position in 2004. She may be reached at obrigk@gwu.edu.

Linda Roscoe is Head of Access Services, Sherrill Library of the Episcopal Divinity School and Lesley University. Linda oversees the circulation, document delivery, and interlibrary loan functions and stack maintenance. A strong interest in e-readers led to a funding proposal with her coauthor to trial an e-reader service. She has an ME from Boston University. She can be reached at lroscoe@lesley.edu.

Carole Thompson, combining years of library systems and information technology experience, a keen interest in the deployment of technology, and the opportunities presented as former Library Director of Texas A&M University's branch campus in Qatar, leverages the benefits of electronic books against the challenges of access and distance. A small campus in the Persian Gulf, Texas A&M University offers engineering programs to Qatari and regional students, combining education and research in a technology-rich environment. Ms. Thompson received her MLIS from the University of California, Berkeley. She also has an MBA from California Lutheran University. Carole is currently employed as the Chief Librarian at the Museum of Islamic Art under the auspices of Qatar Museum Authority in Doha Qatar. She can be reached at cthompson@qma.org.qa.

Meg White is a 20-year veteran of the health sciences publishing industry. Her background includes various sales, marketing, and product development positions at Rittenhouse Book Distributors, Mosby, Williams & Wilkins, and Wolters Kluwer Health/Lippincott Williams & Wilkins. She is a frequent speaker at industry-related conferences on the topics of product development, technology, curriculum, and continuing medical education. Meg is currently Executive Director of Technology Services at Rittenhouse, leveraging her experience in the areas of technology, marketing, product development, and editorial. She headed the development of the company's eBook initiative, the R2 Digital Library, and continues to serve as product manager for the platform. Meg is a past president and former board member of the American Medical Publisher's Association. Meg can be reached at meg.white@rittenhouse.com.

Index